Inhaltsverzeichnis für den Übungsteil

Inhaltsverzeichnis für die Hör-CD (hinten im **Trainingsbuch** eingeklebt)

Gesamtdauer: 48′54″

Vorwort

Liebe Schülerinnen und Schüler,

das neue **Trainingsbuch Schulaufgaben** besteht aus drei Teilen:

1. dem **Übungsteil**,
2. dem **Lösungsheft** mit allen Lösungen,
3. der **Hör-CD** mit den Diktat- und Hörverstehenstexten.

Der **Übungsteil** enthält Übungen zu den folgenden Lernbereichen:

- **Vocabulary**
  mit Übungen zum Wortschatz
- **Grammar**
  mit Übungen zur Grammatik
- **Speaking**
  mit Übungen zum Training der Sprechfertigkeit
- **Writing**
  mit Übungen zur Schulung des Schreibens
- **Mediation**
  mit Übungen zur Übertragung ins Englische
- **Cloze test**
  Texte mit Wortschatzlücken in regelmäßigen Abständen
- **Mixed bag**
  Lückentexte zu Wortschatz und Grammatik
- **Dictation**
  mit Diktatübungen, entweder als ganzes Diktat oder als Lückendiktat
- **Listening**
  mit Übungen zum Hörverstehen

Vor jeder Übung steht, was besonders geübt wird, z. B. **1 Vocabulary: Odd word out.** Möchtet ihr die Grammatik oder das Übertragen ins Englische üben, findet ihr geeignete Übungen unter **Grammar** und **Mediation.** Möchtet ihr noch einen Lückentext üben oder ausprobieren, ob ihr die Vokabeln gut könnt, wählt ihr **Mixed bag, Cloze test** und die Übungen zu **Vocabulary**.

Das **Lösungsheft** enthält alle Seiten des Übungsteils in verkleinerter Form und mit den eingetragenen Lösungen. Hier könnt ihr alle Lösungen schnell und übersichtlich nachschauen. Wenn mehrere Lösungen richtig sind, sind diese auch eingetragen. Bei freien Übungen sind die Lösungen natürlich nur Vorschläge.

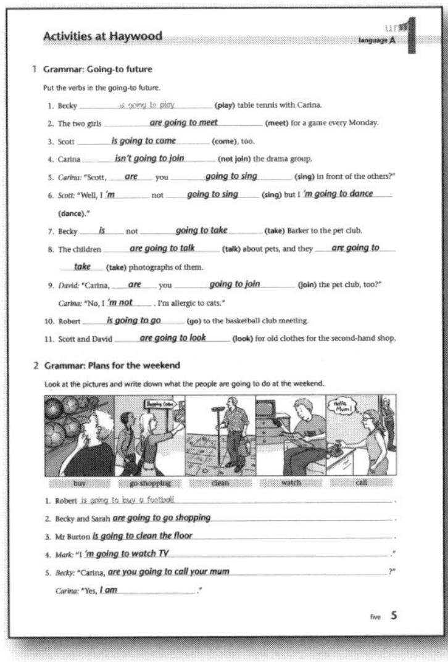

Activities at Haywood — unit 1 language A

1 Grammar: Going-to future

Put the verbs in the going-to future.

1. Becky *is going to play* (play) table tennis with Carina.
2. The two girls *are going to meet* (meet) for a game every Monday.
3. Scott *is going to come* (come), too.
4. Carina *isn't going to join* (not join) the drama group.
5. *Carina:* "Scott, *are* you *going to sing* (sing) in front of the others?"
6. *Scott:* "Well, I *'m* not *going to sing* (sing) but I *'m going to dance* (dance)."
7. Becky *is* not *going to take* (take) Barker to the pet club.
8. The children *are going to talk* (talk) about pets, and they *are going to take* (take) photographs of them.
9. *David:* "Carina, *are* you *going to join* (join) the pet club, too?" *Carina:* "No, I *'m not*. I'm allergic to cats."
10. Robert *is going to go* (go) to the basketball club meeting.
11. Scott and David *are going to look* (look) for old clothes for the second-hand shop.

2 Grammar: Plans for the weekend

Look at the pictures and write down what the people are going to do at the weekend.

buy — go shopping — clean — watch — call

1. Robert *is going to buy a football*.
2. Becky and Sarah *are going to go shopping*.
3. Mr Burton *is going to clean the floor*.
4. *Mark:* "I *'m going to watch TV*."
5. *Becky:* "Carina, *are you going to call your mum*?" *Carina:* "Yes, *I am*."

five 5

Beispielseite aus dem Lösungsheft mit eingetragenen Lösungen

Die **Hör-CD** enthält die Diktate und die Hörverstehenstexte. Die Tracknummer ist bei den jeweiligen Übungen im Übungsteil angegeben. Ihr müsst nur darauf achten, dass ihr die richtige Tracknummer ansteuert. Die vollständigen Diktattexte sind im Lösungsheft abgedruckt. Dort könnt ihr eure Ergebnisse selbst überprüfen. Die Hörverstehenstexte gibt es aber nur auf der CD, denn sie sind ausschließlich zum Hören gedacht.

Das **Trainingsbuch Schulaufgaben** ist genauso aufgebaut wie das Schülerbuch und das **Workbook.** Auf jeder Seite oben ist ein Hinweis, auf welchen Teil des Schülerbuchs sich die Übungen beziehen, z. B. **Unit 2 Language A.**

Diese Gliederung kennt ihr bereits aus dem Schülerbuch und auch aus dem **Workbook**, also nichts Neues für euch.

Natürlich kann man nie ganz genau wissen, was in einer Schulaufgabe wirklich drankommt und jede Lehrerin / jeder Lehrer stellt die Schulaufgaben ein klein wenig anders. Aber für euch ist es wichtig zu wissen, dass alle Lernbereiche, die in den Schulaufgaben vorkommen können, hier im **Trainingsbuch** geübt werden.

Das **Trainingsbuch Schulaufgaben** könnt ihr folgendermaßen benutzen:

1. Zur Vorbereitung auf eine Schulaufgabe: Wenn eure Lehrerin / euer Lehrer z. B. sagt: Die nächste Schulaufgabe geht von Unit 2 bis Unit 3 einschließlich, dann solltet ihr euch im **Trainingsbuch** die Übungen zu Unit 2 und Unit 3 vornehmen und sie möglichst **alle** durcharbeiten. Durch die Anordnung der Übungen könnt ihr sicher sein, dass ihr alle wichtigen Übungsformen mindestens einmal geübt habt. Dann kann eigentlich nichts mehr schief gehen!

2. Zum zusätzlichen Üben zwischen den Schulaufgaben: In diesem Fall könnt ihr nach der Durchnahme eines Abschnitts im Schülerbuch überprüfen, ob ihr den Stoff wirklich beherrscht. Wichtig ist dabei: Das **Trainingsbuch** bitte erst benutzen, **nachdem** ihr den entsprechenden Teil im Schülerbuch durchgenommen habt!

Wie übt ihr am besten?

Am besten übt ihr natürlich regelmäßig und nicht erst kurz vor einer Schulaufgabe. Denn nur so habt ihr Zeit, einen Abschnitt oder einen Lernbereich noch einmal gründlich zu wiederholen, wenn er noch nicht sitzt. Nehmt euch regelmäßig eine oder zwei Übungen vor, sobald ihr ein Kapitel im Schülerbuch abgeschlossen habt. Überprüft mit Hilfe des **Lösungshefts**, ob eure Antworten richtig sind. Es hat aber keinen Zweck, die Lösungen aus dem Lösungsheft abzuschreiben. Ihr könnt mit euren Eltern z. B. vereinbaren, dass ihr das Lösungsheft abgebt und erst hineinschaut, wenn ihr die Übungen durchgeführt habt. Vergleicht dann eure Lösungen mit dem Lösungsheft und verbessert eure Fehler.

Bei allen Übungen, die im Übungsteil ein CD-Symbol am Rand haben, braucht ihr die **Hör-CD**, die hinten im **Trainingsbuch** eingeklebt ist. Hört euch die Hörtexte zunächst immer einmal vollständig an. Lest danach die Aufgabe im Übungsteil durch und hört die Aufnahme ein zweites (und drittes) Mal. Bearbeitet jetzt die Übung und überprüft eure Ergebnisse entweder mit dem Text im Lösungsteil oder hört zur Kontrolle noch einmal die CD.

Wenn einmal ein oder zwei Fehler vorkommen, dann ist das nicht so schlimm. Wenn sich aber die Fehler häufen, dann müsst ihr etwas tun, z. B. noch einmal die Vokabeln lernen oder in der Grammatik im Schülerbuch nachschauen oder die eine oder andere Übung im **Schülerbuch**, **Workbook** oder in der Software **Sprachtrainer Englisch** wiederholen.

Wir wünschen euch viel Erfolg mit dem **Trainingsbuch Schulaufgaben.**

unit 1 intro

Back to school

1 Grammar: Simple past

Put the verbs in the simple past.

David ___had___ **(have)** a lot of fun in the holidays. He __________ **(go)** to New York with his parents and __________ **(visit)** his aunt and his cousin. Aunt Meg __________ **(meet)** them at the airport and __________ **(drive)** them to her apartment. After dinner David and Mary-Beth __________ **(play)** computer games. On their second day Aunt Meg __________ **(show)** them the skyscrapers of Manhattan and they __________ **(stand)** on the roof of the Empire State Building. In the evening they __________ **(watch)** an American football game. Two of Mary-Beth's friends __________ **(come)** with them. After the game the children __________ **(talk)** about the teams and David's new friends __________ **(tell)** him a lot of interesting things about American football. They ________________ **(not go)** to a baseball game because the team __________ **(not be)** in New York that week. David __________ **(buy)** some souvenirs of New York and __________ **(take)** lots of photos. He __________ **(write)** postcards to his friends in England, but he only __________ **(send)** some of them.

He __________ **(carry)** the postcard to his best friend Robert in his pocket until the end of the trip! When they __________ **(be)** back home in Nottingham, David __________ **(give)** Robert the postcard and they both __________ **(laugh)**. The other children __________ **(get)** their postcards two days later!

2 Vocabulary: Profile

Put in the missing words.

Name__________________ : Glen Parker

____________________ : 12

____________________ : British

____________________ : 22 Court Road, London

____________________ : Football, computers

____________________ : Leeds United, chocolate

____________________ : Bullies, fish and chips

______________________________ : Robbie Williams

______________________________ : One sister (Kate), 10

Activities at Haywood

1 Grammar: Going-to future

Put the verbs in the going-to future.

1. Becky _____is going to play_____ **(play)** table tennis with Carina.
2. The two girls ______________________ **(meet)** for a game every Monday.
3. Scott ______________________ **(come)**, too.
4. Carina ______________________ **(not join)** the drama group.
5. *Carina:* "Scott, __________ you ______________________ **(sing)** in front of the others?"
6. *Scott:* "Well, I __________ not ______________________ **(sing)** but I ______________________ **(dance)**."
7. Becky __________ not ______________________ **(take)** Barker to the pet club.
8. The children ______________________ **(talk)** about pets, and they ______________________ **(take)** photographs of them.
9. *David:* "Carina, __________ you ______________________ **(join)** the pet club, too?"
   Carina: "No, I __________ . I'm allergic to cats."
10. Robert ______________________ **(go)** to the basketball club meeting.
11. Scott and David ______________________ **(look)** for old clothes for the second-hand shop.

2 Grammar: Plans for the weekend

Look at the pictures and write down what the people are going to do at the weekend.

buy | go shopping | clean | watch | call

1. Robert _is going to buy a football_______________________.
2. Becky and Sarah ______________________________________.
3. Mr Burton ______________________________________.
4. *Mark:* "I ______________________________________."
5. *Becky:* "Carina, ______________________________________?"
   Carina: "Yes, ______________________."

3 Speaking: A new boy at Haywood School

Put in the question tags. Give short answers and correct the wrong statements.

1. Nice weather today, isn't it ? Yes, it is .
2. You're new here, ______ ? Yes, ______ .
3. Your name is David, ______ ? No, ______ . ______ Scott.
4. You're not American, ______ ? Yes, ______ .
5. Americans like fast food, ______ ? Well, most Americans ______ . But I ______ .
6. But you can play basketball, ______ ? Yes, ______ , but I'm not very good.
7. You live in Sherwood, ______ ? Yes, ______ .
8. Your dad works here, ______ ? Yes, ______ .
9. You've got a brother, ______ ? No, ______ . ______ a sister.
10. You came here by plane, ______ ? Yes, of course ______ !
11. You were here last year, ______ ? No, ______ !
12. You don't talk much, ______ ? Well, not always. But sometimes I ______ .
13. You're not angry, ______ ? Well, … not really.
14. But you'd like to go now, ______ ? Yes, ______ . Bye!

4 Mediation: At a British school

Stell dir vor, du bist zu Besuch an einer englischen Schule. Was sagst du auf Englisch, wenn …

1. … dir gerade jemand vorgestellt worden ist?

______

2. … du meinst, dass viel los ist an dieser Schule?

______

3. … du etwas schade findest?

______

4. … du jemanden wissen lassen willst, dass du leider nicht einer Meinung mit ihm / ihr bist?

______

5. … du jemanden fragen willst, warum er / sie sich nicht der Theatergruppe anschließt?

______

6. … du jemanden fragen willst, ob er / sie etwas sucht?

______

7. … du jemandem mitteilen willst, dass du niesen musst, wenn eine Katze in deiner Nähe ist?

______

Drama at the drama club

1 Grammar: Past progressive

On Sunday Becky took Barker for a walk in the park.
What was happening when Becky and Barker arrived at the park?

1. Two girls ___were dancing___ .
2. A girl ______ a book.
3. A boy ______ his bike.
4. Two girls ______ football.
5. A woman ______ under a tree.
6. A boy ______ in the grass[1].
7. A man ______ an ice cream.
8. Two dogs ______ a cat.

[1] [grɑːs] – Gras

2 Grammar: Simple past or past progressive?

Put the verbs in the correct tense.

Yesterday Robert and David ___were playing___ **(play)** football when it ___started___ **(start)** to rain. While they ______ **(walk)** home, the rain ______ **(stop)**, but they ______ **(not want)** to stay outside. When they ______ **(arrive)** at the Penroses' house, Mark ______ **(sit)** in the living room. He ______ **(watch)** TV. David ______ **(say)** to him: "Please go to your room, Mark!" But Mark ______ **(not answer)**. So David ______ **(try)** it again: "Hey, Mark, didn't you hear what I said?" But Mark ______ **(stay)** where he ______ **(be)**. This ______ **(make)** David really angry, but then Robert ______ **(have)** an idea: "Let's play your new computer game!" – "Great idea!"

3 Mediation: What a great show!

Write down what happened in the drama club.

1. Viele Leute schauten zu, als die Kinder in der Theatergruppe zeigten, was sie können.

   A lot of people were watching while the kids in the drama club were showing what they could do.

2. Aber alles ging schief!

   ____

3. Ein Mädchen stolperte über das Bein ihres Partners, während sie tanzten.

   ____

   ____

4. Ein anderes Mädchen sang gerade ein Lied, als jemand von seinem Stuhl fiel.

   ____

   ____

5. Also hörte sie auf, weil alle lachten.

   ____

6. Während ein Junge einen Witz erzählte, warf er sein Handy einem anderen Jungen zu.

   ____

   ____

7. Aber der andere Junge fing es nicht – er ließ es fallen!

   ____

4 Vocabulary: Prepositions

Put in the right prepositions.

1. Do you do your homework ___in___ the afternoon?
2. In the holidays we were ________ the seaside.
3. Sarah and Becky showed Carina ________ their school.
4. Wayne and Barry fell ________ their skateboard.
5. The skateboard flew ________ the stage.
6. I talked to him ________ the telephone.
7. My birthday is ________ March 17th.
8. Let's meet ________ lunchtime!

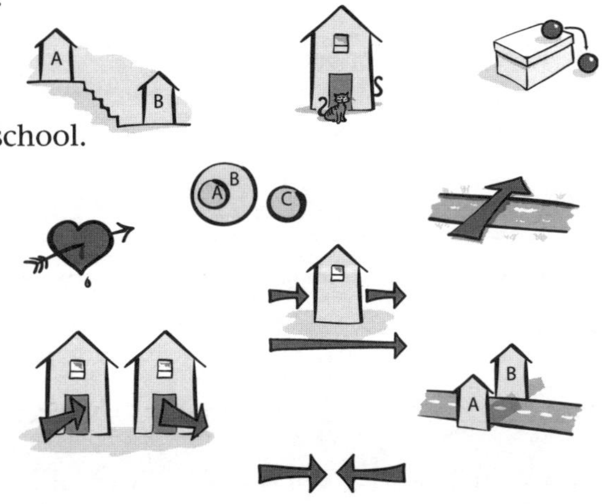

The champion

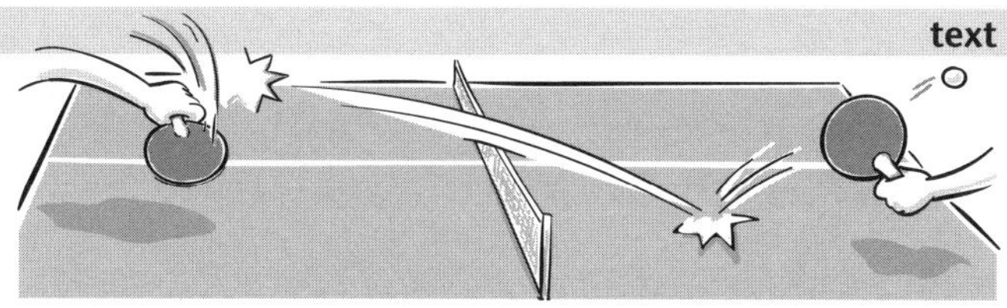

1 Cloze test: A bully

Fill in the gaps.

When Carina plays table tennis ______________ her brother, she sometimes wins and sometimes ______________ . At Haywood the kids can play at the ______________ centre. While Carina and Becky ______________ playing there in the lunch ______________ last Monday, Wayne and his nasty ______________ came in. "Girls, it's our ______________ now," said Wayne and ______________ the bat from Becky. Carina ______________ to help her friend, but Barry ______________ her away. Then the boys got ______________ to play. "We don't want any ______________ with them," said Becky. "Wayne ______________ it's his table because ______________ is in the school table tennis ______________ ."

Carina was watching Wayne and Barry ______________ they were playing. Wayne sometimes ______________ the ball so hard that Barry ______________ it. Then Carina went back ______________ the table. "You're not ______________ the racket right, boy!" she ______________ Wayne. "Racket? This is a bat! ______________ girls know anything about sport?"

2 Writing: A great game

Match the parts of the sentences and write them down.

1. Carina grabbed Barry's bat	**but**	Carina made a joke.
2. Wayne ran,	**because**	they wanted to watch.
3. The other kids stopped their games	**while**	she won the game.
4. I missed the ball	**when**	they weren't good enough.
5. Everybody laughed	**so**	people were making so much noise.
6. Wayne tried a lot of tricks,	**but**	he was waiting for Wayne's return.
7. Carina was too good for Wayne,	**because**	the ball was too fast for him.

1. Carina grabbed Barry's bat while he was waiting for Wayne's return.
2. ______________
3. ______________
4. ______________
5. ______________
6. ______________
7. ______________

3 Grammar: Word order

Put the verbs in the simple past or the past progressive and use ***when*** or ***while***.

1. Becky • a • **(run)** • the • she • CD • park • **(listen to)** • in

Becky was listening to a CD while she was running in the park.

2. Scott • **(meet)** • school • he • home • **(walk)** • Wayne • from

3. Sarah • mobile • her • **(do)** • her • Jenny • **(call)** • homework • on • her

4. Robert • his • **(fall)** • he • arm • **(break)** • bike • off • his

5. David • noise • a • **(read)** • a • **(hear)** • book • he

6. Mark • in • room • **(play)** • his • **(watch)** • parents • TV • his

4 Dictation: Carina is from Bavaria

1 Listen to track 1 and write the sentences.

1 Vocabulary: Useful phrases

Put in the missing words.

1. "You are Becky, aren't you ?" – " Actually , I'm Sarah."
2. "How are you?" – "__________, thanks. And you?"
3. "__________ you like something to drink?" – "Yes, please."
4. "Can I use your mobile, please?" – "Yes, of course. __________ you are."
5. "Atishoo!" – "__________ you!"
6. "I'm in year 8." – "__________ too."
7. "We wear school uniform." – "Really? __________ it like? Is it nice?"
8. "Did you __________ a good holiday?" – "No, I didn't! It was terrible."

2 Speaking: Question tags

Say it in English and use question tags.

1. Du interessierst dich für Basketball, nicht wahr?
   You're interested in basketball, aren't you?
2. Sarah ist nicht der Theatergruppe beigetreten, oder?
   ____
3. Carina ist zu Besuch an unserer Schule, stimmt's?
   ____
4. Scott hat ein tolles Skateboard, nicht wahr?
   ____
5. Wir können mittags Tischtennis spielen, oder?
   ____

3 Grammar: Simple past or past progressive?

Put in the correct verb forms.

Yesterday Sarah was riding **(ride)** her bike when she saw **(see)** Scott. He __________ **(talk)** to another boy. "Hello Scott!" Sarah __________ **(say)**, but Scott __________ **(not hear)** her because he __________ **(shout)** at the other boy. Sarah __________ **(get)** off her bike and __________ **(go)** over to the two boys. When Scott __________ **(see)** her, he __________ **(stop)** shouting. While Scott __________ **(tell)** Sarah why he was so angry, the other boy __________ **(watch)** them. Suddenly he __________ **(run)** away.

1 focus

Focus on Halloween

1 Writing: Tips for trick-or-treating

Fill in the missing words and match the parts of the sentences.

1. Always go in ___groups___
2. Never go into ______ houses
3. ______ right and left
4. Explain how you want to ______ the money
5. ______ friendly and thank everybody

a) to ______ other people.
b) and take an ______ with you.
c) when they give you money or ______ .
d) because you don't ______ what's inside.
e) before you go ______ the street.

2 Writing: The history of Halloween

Write two short texts about the history of Halloween. Use the given words and think of good verbs.

1. Celtic • Ireland • end of summer • October 31st • scary • ghosts

______

______

______

2. Christians • village • November 2nd • soul cakes • prayer

______

______

______

3 Listening: The end of Grandpa's ghost story?

2 Listen to track 2 and complete the sentences.

The barn went ______ ______ ______ .

Our masks were lying ______ ______ ______ .

We're going to wait for the ghost to ______ ______ ______ wall here. Somebody was ______ ______ the barn. Suddenly, somebody in a red mask came into ______ ______ ______ the lantern. It was the farmer, and he ______ ______ ______ . Next day I went back to the field, and the barn ______ ______ .

Robin Hood country

unit 2 intro

1 Vocabulary: Crossword

Across →

4. A lot of people have tea or ... for breakfast.
6. Singers need it on stage, so that people can hear them.
8. If you can't ... what a country is like, you must go and see it. If you can't ... what a person is like, you must meet him or her.
10. The number, the street and the place where you live.
12. Opposite of 'child'.

Down ↓

1. What a lot of people do on their birthday.
2. A huge vegetable. People put a light in it on Halloween.
3. "Why don't you ... our tennis club? Then we can play tennis together every week."
5. People in church usually sing and say ... together.
7. Another word for 'to get (lunch, breakfast etc.) ready'.
9. Opposite of 'nice' (when you speak about a person).
11. To bring the ball into play (at tennis or table tennis).

2 Grammar: Simple form or progressive form?

Every morning Sarah ______ gets ______ **(get)** up at six o'clock. But not yesterday. Yesterday she ____________ **(be)** late. When the alarm clock ____________ **(wake)** her up for the second time, she ____________ **(still, lie)** in bed. But then she ____________ **(jump)** out of bed and ____________ **(run)** into the bathroom and afterwards she ____________ **(hurry)** into the kitchen. While she ____________ **(stand)** at the bus stop, she ____________ **(see)** Becky in a car. Her father ____________ **(drive)** her to school. They ____________ **(stop)**.

Sarah: "I have missed my bus. Now I ____________ **(be)** late."

Becky: "____________ **(not worry)**. We ____________ **(can, take)** you to school in our car."

1 Grammar: Comparisons

Make three different comparisons for each picture.

strong

powerful

good runners

happy

dangerous

bad teams

1. Bill is stronger than Benjamin, but he is not as strong as Bully. Bully is the strongest of the three.

2. The Mercedes is ____________ the Mini, but it isn't ____________ ____________ the Ferrari. The Ferrari is ____________ of the three.

3. Tim is ____________ George, but he isn't ____________ ____________ Joe. Joe is ____________ of the three.

4. ____

5. ____

6. ____

2 Grammar: Texas is best!

Bud, a boy from Texas, visits David in Nottingham. They go to the Sherwood Forest Visitor Centre together with David's friend Paul. Bud thinks that everything is better in Texas. Fill in the correct form of the adjective.

tip
= Gleichheit
\+ Komparativ (Ungleichheit)
– Komparativ (Ungleichheit, verneint)
++ Superlativ

Paul: Where in Texas are you from, Bud?

Bud: I'm from Dallas, the **(beautiful ++)** most beautiful city in the USA.

It has also got the **(busy ++)** ____________ airport in the world.

Paul: But I think New York has **(good +)** ______________ and also **(high +)** ______________ skyscrapers than Dallas. And Dallas is **(big –)** ______________ New York. New York is a much ______________ **(exciting +)** city.

Bud: I'm sure people in New York are **(friendly –)** ______________ people in Texas. They also drive a lot **(bad +)** ______________ Texans and their cars are much **(small +)** ______________ our cars.

Paul: Oh, come on! For you cars are **(important +)** ______________ anything else. I think cars are **(boring ++)** ______________ thing in the world.

David: Your hobby is planes. I think cars are just **(interesting =)** ______________ planes. But let's watch that film about Robin Hood now, England's **(famous ++)** ______________ folk hero. He still is **(popular +)** ______________ anybody else here in England.

3 Mediation: In English, please

1. Die sächsischen Kleinbauern waren ärmer als die meisten Normannen.

   The Saxon peasants were poorer than most of the Normans.

2. Jeder weiß, dass Robin Hood schlauer als der Sheriff von Nottingham war.

   ____

3. Er ist immer noch der berühmteste Volksheld in England.

   ____

4. Für England ist er genau so wichtig wie Wilhelm Tell für die Schweiz (= *Switzerland*).

   ____

5. Heute ist das Leben in Nottingham nicht ganz so aufregend wie im Mittelalter.

   ____

6. Aber Nottingham wird immer beliebter bei (= *with*) Touristen.

   ____

1 Grammar: About sports

Write about the different people in the pictures. Make sentences with ***who*** or ***whose***.
Start with ***There is … / There are …***

1. There are a boy and a girl whose hobby is football.
2. There are some girls ______
3. There is ______
4. ______
5. ______
6. ______
7. ______
8. ______

2 Mediation: A pop concert

Stephanie went to a pop concert last week. She wants to tell her English friend what happened there.

1. Das Konzert, auf das ich letzte Woche ging, war toll.

The concert (that / which) I went to last week was great.

2. Viele Leute, die ich dort traf, kamen von weit her.

______

3. Ein Mädchen, mit dem ich einige Zeit sprach, kam aus Deutschland.

4. Ich mochte die Lieder, die die irische Gruppe sang.

5. Die Fotos, die meine Freundin machte, waren schrecklich.

6. Hier sind die Fotos, die ich von dem Konzert in der Zeitung gefunden habe.

7. Die Eintrittskarte, die mir meine Eltern zum Geburtstag kauften, kostete 15 Pfund.

3 Grammar: Contact clause

Lewis is visiting Nottingham and sends texts from his mobile to his friends. He uses contact clauses in all his sentences. Start with the underlined words.

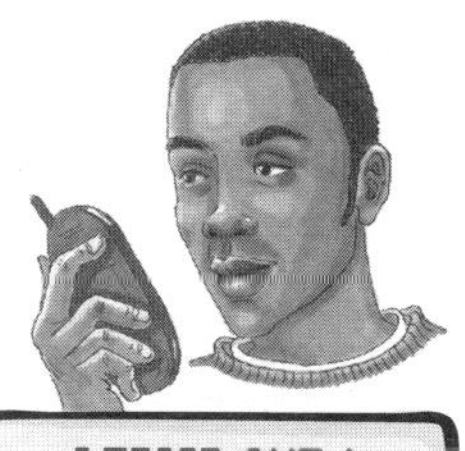

THEY HAVE A FANTASTIC FOREST HERE.

YOU CAN SEE A HUGE OLD OAK IN THIS FOREST.

WE WENT TO A MOST INTERESTING VISITOR CENTRE.

I TRIED OUT A REALLY GREAT HISTORIC LONGBOW.

THEY SELL INTERESTING SOUVENIRS OF NOTTINGHAM THERE.

THEY SHOW A QUITE BORING VIDEO ON KING JOHN.

YOU CAN BUY NICE POSTERS OF ROBIN HOOD THERE.

BUT SOMEONE MADE A VERY STUPID JOKE ABOUT MY BASEBALL CAP[1].

1. The forest they have here is fantastic.
2. The old oak
3.
4.
5.
6.
7.
8.

[1] [kæp] – Kappe, Mütze

Robin Hood and the silver arrow

1 Speaking: Looking at photos

Sarah and Pat are looking at the photos of their trip to London. Use contact clauses.

Sarah: the boy (we / meet / station)
Pat: the girl (we / see / zoo)
Sarah: the man (we / talk to / Trafalgar Square)
Pat: the people (Betty / ask for the way)
Sarah: the statue (Sandra / take a photo of / near Big Ben)
Pat: the two guides (some tourists / joke about / the Tower / because they were so funny)

Sarah: Look, this is the boy we met ______________________

Pat: ______________________

Sarah: ______________________

Pat: ______________________

Sarah: ______________________

____

Pat: ______________________

____

2 Dictation: Haywood School Drama Group

3 Listen to track 3 and complete the text.

Haywood School has a ____________ drama group. Sometimes the boys and girls in the group find a play ____________ and act it. But ____________ plays, too. They find a ____________ with ____________ and write the dialogues for them. Sometimes they are very ____________ and ____________ ____________.

Then they ____________ the ____________ people ____________. In some of their plays they need lots of people ____________. Some people in the drama group don't want ____________ in every play, but ____________ with the stage ____________.

One year there was a Schools' Drama ____________ with ____________. The Haywood drama group ____________ it, but they ____________ and they were ____________. The drama group plays are ____________ very ____________ and ____________ of people go to watch them.

3 Vocabulary: Words in disguise

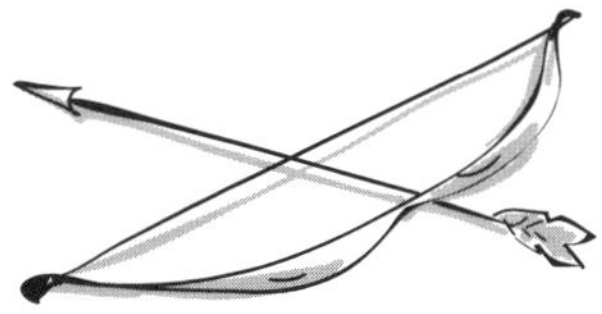

Find ten words that have to do with Robin Hood's favourite sport. Mark them and write them down in alphabetical order.

w	e	a	t	h	c	r	o	w	d	c	k
x	c	f	g	h	l	v	h	i	m	p	f
h	d	s	a	n	r	o	u	n	d	h	n
g	x	p	r	f	g	h	l	n	s	x	t
h	f	d	c	r	e	s	s	e	d	s	a
m	i	x	h	o	b	t	a	r	g	e	t
j	n	e	e	d	o	a	c	r	j	g	f
u	a	r	r	o	w	h	y	p	s	o	l
d	l	o	y	v	o	c	x	y	h	s	d
u	w	i	n	d	k	g	b	o	o	t	f
s	c	o	m	p	e	t	i	t	o	r	i
e	f	n	s	u	n	s	c	r	t	e	n

1. __________
2. __________
3. __________
4. __________
5. __________
6. __________
7. __________
8. __________
9. __________
10. __________

Now check if Robin Hood's favourite sport is the first word on your list.

4 Listening: Drama at Haywood School

4 Listen to track 4 and answer the questions.

1. What did the drama group write and act?

2. What did the king do in Sherwood Forest?

3. What did Robin Hood do with the money from the rich people?

4. What colour did the outlaws wear in Sherwood Forest?

5. What part did Mr Cooper act?

6. What were the Haywood outlaws carrying in the school play?

7. What role does Mr Cooper like better than the part of the Sheriff of Nottingham?

1 Vocabulary: Word power

1. The plural of **wife** is ____________, the plural of **woman** is ____________.
2. **Worse** is the comparative, and **worst** is the ____________.
3. A man and a woman who love one another usually ____________ after some time.

   But some people never do. They want to stay alone.
4. When you have a really great appetite you can say: I'm ____________.
5. The adjective is **different** and ____________ is the noun.
6. When you shoot an arrow you want to hit the ____________.
7. When you meet a person for the first time you can say: ____________!

2 Writing: Explaining words

Put the correct parts together and link them. Use a relative pronoun or make a contact clause.

1. stage	information	show you around and …
2. show-off	person	buy things for little money
3. table tennis	place	play on a table with a …
4. hall	game	people act plays
5. Physial Education	room	teach sports to …
6. bully	person	tell everybody how good …
7. second-hand shop	place	like it if others are scared of …
8. guide	subject	get from others about …
9. feedback	person	meet for assembly or …

1. A stage is a place where people act plays.
2. ____________
3. ____________
4. ____________
5. ____________
6. ____________
7. ____________
8. ____________
9. ____________

1 Grammar: Word order

Make positive statements (+), negative statements (–) or questions (?).
Use the correct tense: present or past, simple or progressive form.

1. (+) tea • **(have)** • usually • for breakfast • Barbara • coffee • but today • **(have)** • she

____

____

2. (–) David's • **(learn)** • at school • **(be)** • young • French • when • mother • she

____

____

3. (?) Janet • yesterday • **(not go)** • to school • by bike • why

____

4. (?) you • **(think)** • that • **(learn)** • Latin • be • difficult

____

5. (+) my father • **(try)** • his • Look • new mobile • **(use)**

____

2 Mixed bag: From David's history book

Fill in the missing words.

_____ 1066 the Normans _______________ England. Some time later, around 1190, Nottingham was a small English _______________ of about a thousand _______________. Sometimes they were hungry _______________ they didn't have the right to hunt _______________ in the forest. When the King _______________ money, cruel[1] sheriffs usually _______________ it for him. Some Saxons couldn't _______________, so the sheriffs quite often _______________ all their goods and homes. So the peasants _______________ outlaws. The most _______________ of them was Robin Hood. He lived in Sherwood _______________ with a group of strong men. They _______________ money from the _______________ people of Nottingham and _______________ it to the _______________ families. Two hundred years _______________, people began to _______________ the first stories _______________ Robin Hood. And today _______________ still learn about _________ in schools.

[1] [krʊəl] – grausam

Sounds good

1 Cloze test: What music do they like?

Complete the text with the following words.

all | are | band | bands' | dancing | different | doesn't | film | forty | got | great | Guitars | Her | His | is | likes | lot | music | not | Scott | She | she | their | they | three | to | when

Sarah's favourite _____ is Atomic Kitten. They are _____ girls from Liverpool who first _____ together in 1999. They had _____ first international hit in 2001. David _____ rock, anything with guitars. _____ are very important to him. _____ favourite band is U2. It _____ matter to him that they _____ already quite old. He thinks their singer, Bono, has a _____ voice. 'Elevation' is the song _____ did for the Lara Croft _____. Robert isn't very interested in _____, so he never knows the _____ names. He just likes football. _____ likes to listen to hip-hop. He thinks it's great for _____, but also for saying a _____ of things that you need _____ say. Mrs Dane's favourite music _____ jazz. She didn't like it _____ she was young, but now _____ thinks it's fantastic. There are _____ kinds of jazz and they _____ use different kinds of instruments, _____ only guitar, bass and drums. _____ actually likes the saxophone best. _____ favourite song is already over _____ years old, but she still thinks it's great.

2 Vocabulary: Funny words

Can you find the words?

1. **ieecpeerxn** experience
2. **pistpoeo** _____
3. **zenese** _____
4. **ehtlha** _____
5. **hcuborer** _____
6. **deaefkcb** _____
7. **ldsikie** _____
8. **htyirso** _____
9. **naemngi** _____
10. **eduig** _____
11. **icplayhs** _____
12. **ncteiudoa** _____

Two events

1 Grammar: *Will* or *won't*?

There is a match between Nottingham Forest and Arsenal on Friday. The Forest manager is worried. Put in *will* or *won't*.

The weather report says the weather __________ be bad on Friday. I hope it __________ rain all day. Too much rain __________ ruin the grass[1] on the football field because the ground __________ become soft[2]. And lots of people __________ come if they know they __________ get wet. If the fans stay at home, we __________ have the money to pay our players.

I know that most of the Arsenal fans __________ come by train and of course, they __________ make a lot of noise in the city. I hope our fans __________ get too excited when they see them. I'm sure we __________ win, but what __________ the fans do if we lose?

[1] [grɑːs] – Gras • [2] [sɒft] – weich

2 Grammar: The second ticket

Complete the dialogue with *will* or *won't* and mark the signal words.

tip

Signal words for the ***will future***

I expect	I'm sure
I hope	perhaps
I think	I'm afraid

Sarah: (Do you think) Robert __________ go to the concert with me? I'm afraid he __________ laugh at me when I ask him.

Becky: Don't be silly, Sarah. I expect he __________ be surprised when you ask him, but he __________ laugh at you. I know he likes you.

Sarah: Perhaps he __________ have time.

Becky: Maybe, but I think he __________ tell you, __________ he?

Sarah: I expect he __________ watch the football match on TV. He's a big fan.

Becky: Come on, Sarah, here's my mobile. Ring him up. You __________ find out what he thinks if you don't ask him.

Sarah: Oh Becky, I hope he __________ make fun of me.

3 Grammar: Plans for Friday

Write down what they are going to do next Friday.

celebrate

watch

listen to

do

1. The Burtons ______________________________ Grandma's birthday.
2. Robert ______________________________
3. Sarah and Kim ______________________________
4. Mr Burton ______________________________

4 Grammar: A Robin Hood film

Fill in the correct tenses: present and past, simple or progressive form.

Yesterday Mum and I ______________ **(watch)** a silly Robin Hood film on TV. The best scene ______________ **(be)** when the outlaws ______________ **(hide)** in the forest. Some of them ______________ **(lie)** under the bushes, others ______________ **(sit)** in the trees when they ______________ **(see)** Maid Marian. She ______________ **(ride)** on a horse and ______________ **(sing)** a song, but then she ______________ **(hear)** a noise in a tree above her and a hat ______________ **(fall)** down from the tree. She ______________ **(pick up)** the hat, ______________ **(put)** it on her head at once and ______________ **(shout)**, "Robin, I ______________ **(know)** it's you! Where ______________ **(you hide)**? Look, what I ______________ **(buy)** in Nottingham yesterday!" She ______________ **(give)** him a little dog. "I ______________ **(think)** it will be useful in our camp," she ______________ **(say)**. Then the outlaws ______________ **(come)** out of the trees. We ______________ **(laugh)** because they ______________ **(look)** so funny. They ______________ **(not look)** real at all. Their bows and arrows ______________ **(be)** modern. Maybe they ______________ **(get)** them from a toy[1] shop.

[1] [tɔɪ] – Spielzeug

Sarah's second ticket

1 Grammar: At the Burtons'

There is a lot of work to do before Grandma's birthday party, but everybody is friendly and will help. Use the ***will future*** for snap decisions.

Jobs to do
- make birthday cake ✔
- decorate living room
- not forget to give Grandma the present
- buy drinks
- invite neighbours
- go for a walk with Barker
- set table
- collect Aunt Mary at station
- not tell Grandma anything

Decide who of the Burtons wants to do what job. Start with:
All right, I'll ... • Don't worry, ... • Of course, ... • OK, ...

Mum: All right, I'll make the birthday cake.

Dad: ______

Becky and Simon: ______

Simon: ______

Mum: ______

Dad: ______

Becky: ______

Simon: ______

Becky: ______

2 Speaking: Questions

1. Peter was looking for his ... . What was Peter looking for?
2. Carina comes from ... . Where ______?
3. She is going to look after ... . Who ______?
4. The boys are interested in ... . What ______?
5. He went to the cinema with ... . Who ______?
6. Simon never plays with ... . Who ______?

1 Writing: You choose

Write the correct sentences.
Put the letters of the sentences in these boxes.

1. Do you do **(F)** / Will you do **(C)** / Are you going to do **(A)** anything interesting this evening?

   Are you going to do anything interesting this evening?

2. I'm going to **(U)** / I'll **(P)** listen to a pop concert tonight.

   _____

3. I hope Jim will go **(T)** / goes **(L)** / is going to go **(V)** with me to the concert.

   _____

4. Are you sure the train arrives **(I)** / will arrive **(O)** / is going to arrive **(D)** in time?

   _____

5. How many people will we **(B)** / are we going to **(G)** / do we **(D)** invite to our party?

   _____

6. I'm sure Harry doesn't **(S)** / won't **(R)** isn't going to **(A)** come anyway.

   _____

7. Steve can't meet us now. He's working **(A)** / works **(G)** / is going to work **(S)**.

   _____

8. Don't worry, I'm going to phone **(H)** / I'll phone **(P)** / I'm phoning **(U)** you soon.

   _____

9. Do you think Jane is inviting **(T)** / invites **(V)** / will invite **(H)** us, too?

   _____

2 Dictation: Mr Penrose's e-mail to Mrs Croft

5 Listen to track 5 and complete the text.

Dear Sue,

This is _____ for you and Robert. We _____ a garden party _____ in Arndale Road. It _____ at _____, on Saturday 24th. We _____ at 2.30 pm. The party is _____ Jenny Leinert _____, Helen and Martin. _____, Jenny stayed with us _____ while _____ in Berlin. Helen Leinert is _____. _____ in Nottingham. The _____ tutor group, so it's nice to know _____, too. We hope the _____ will be fine for the party and that you and Robert _____.

See you there, Colin Penrose

3 Mediation: In English, please

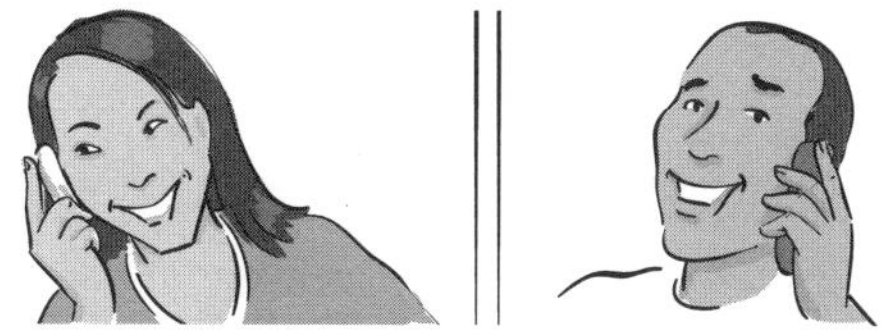

Remember that you often need future forms in English for German *'Präsens'*.

1. Kim begrüßt Lewis und teilt ihm mit, dass sie gerade am Schreibtisch sitzt und sich auf den Mathetest am Dienstag vorbereitet.
2. Lewis hofft, dass er nicht zu schwer sein wird. Er sagt, dass er letzte Woche einen Englischtest hatte und dass er OK war.
3. Sie fragt ihn, was er am Mittwochnachmittag macht. Sie möchte gern ins Kino gehen und fragt ihn, ob er auch mitkommen kann.
4. Lewis bedauert, dass er (da) nicht kann, weil er mittwochs immer Bandprobe (= *practice*) hat. Er schlägt vor, am Donnerstag ins Kino zu gehen.
5. Kim hält das für eine gute Idee und entscheidet spontan nachzuschauen, welche Filme dann laufen (= *to be on*). Sie wird ihn später wieder anrufen. Sie verabschiedet sich.

1. ______________________________
____
2. ______________________________
____
3. ______________________________
____
____
4. ______________________________
____
____
5. ______________________________
____
____

4 Listening: Interview with a pop singer

6 Listen to track 6 and put the sentences in the right order.

1. you • Britain • like • don't • you

You ______________________________

2. Nottingham • fans • my • it's • all • for • in

It's ______________________________

3. Saturday • concert • a • it's • special • on

It's ______________________________

4. Robin • concert • the • at • Hood • I'm • won't • be • afraid

I'm afraid ______________________________

5. six • I'm • back • morning • fly • going • on • at • to • Monday • o'clock

I'm ______________________________

6. longbow • a • take • to • I'm • back • going

I'm ______________________________

1 Speaking: Sound practice

Put the words in the right list.

also • appetite • archery • at last • at least • behind • buy • corpse • darkness • decide • detail • each • final • laugh • outlaw • piece • repeat • saw • strawberry • target

art [ɑ:t]	**leave** [li:v]	**order** [ɔ:də]	**hide** [haɪd]
archery			

2 Vocabulary: Puzzle time

Fill in the words.

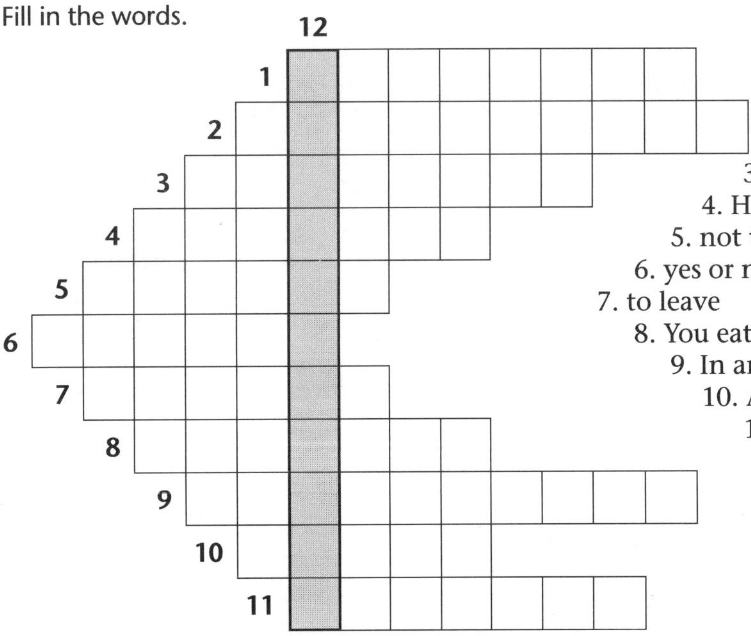

1. almost sure, more than perhaps
2. what you tell about the future
3. You do it for homework.
4. He plays in a band.
5. not the general information but …
6. yes or no, you must …
7. to leave
8. You eat it after the main course.
9. In an art … you see a lot of paintings.
10. A … of chocolate, please.
11. e.g. I – you – he
12. The Arsenal team wants to win it.

3 Vocabulary: Definitions

Use relative clauses or contact clauses and put in ***person – dish – place – list – boy or girl.***

1. A **takeaway** is a place which / that sells meals (which / that) you can take home with you.
2. A **menu** ______________________
3. A **waiter** ______________________
4. The **dessert** ______________________
5. A **pupil** ______________________

Focus on food and drink

1 Mediation: Lunch at the Burtons'

Write down what they say.

- Mrs Burton fragt Carina, ob sie etwas Suppe möchte.
- Carina stimmt zu und sagt, dass sie prima riecht.
- Mr Burton bittet höflich um das Salz.
- Becky reicht es ihm.
- Simon bittet höflich um mehr Reis.
- Mrs Burton ermuntert ihn, sich selbst zu nehmen.
- Becky fragt Carina, ob sie ihr noch mehr Fisch geben kann.
- Carina lehnt höflich ab, weil sie nicht sehr hungrig ist.
- Simon bietet spontan an, dass er den Nachtisch holt. Er fragt, wer etwas Eis möchte.

Mrs Burton: Would you like some soup, Carina?

Carina: ______________________________

Mr Burton: ______________________________

Becky: ______________________________

Simon: ______________________________

Mrs Burton: ______________________________

Becky: ______________________________

Carina: ______________________________

Simon: ______________________________

2 Vocabulary: A crossword puzzle

Across →

1. another word for 'very surprised'
4. a plan you make for the future, often with someone else
6. opposite of the noun 'light'
11. a small book in which you write something down every day
12. to say something again
13. a small word like 'in', 'after', 'at' or 'under'

Down ↓

2. This is how you feel if you hope something will happen, but it doesn't.
3. the first part, e.g. of a text
5. comparative of 'bad'
7. things you throw away
8. At an art ... you can see lots of different pictures or paintings.
9. What will the weather be like tomorrow? – It'll ... rain in the afternoon.
10. the person or team that is in front of all the others

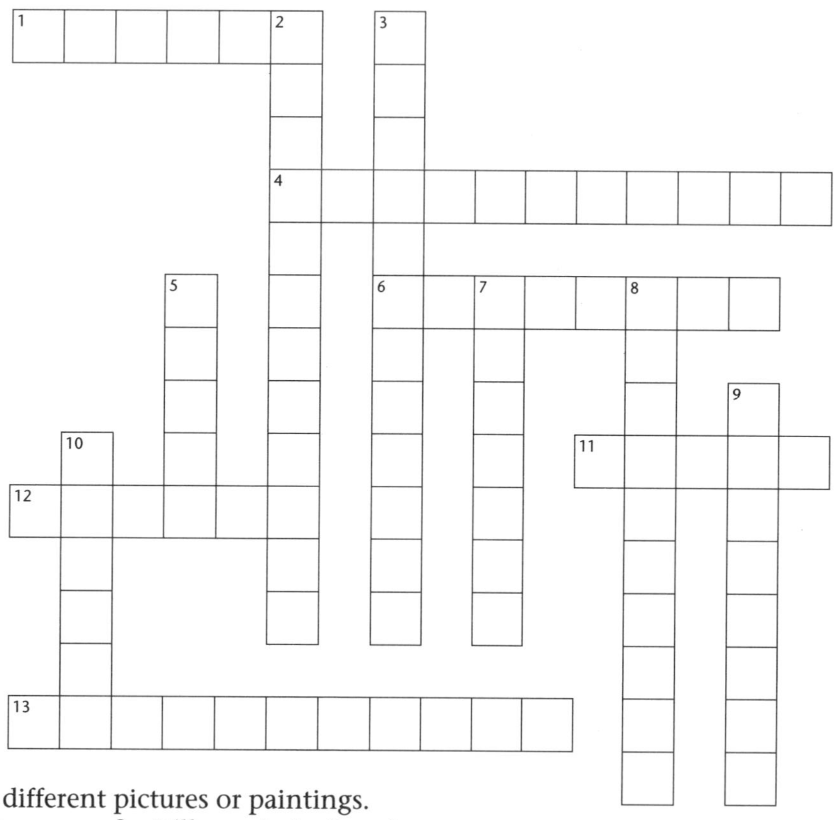

unit 4 intro

A week in the Lake District

1 Cloze test: A week in the Lake District

Put in the missing words.

Jenny __________ to the Lake District in the ______________ holidays with her _________________ and David. Before they left, they ______________ a lot of things and then _____________ couldn't get everthing into the __________. When Jenny was back home, she made a _____________________. She put all the photos _______________ it and this is what she wrote: "We stayed at a ___________ and ____________________ place. One afternoon we ______________ rowing on Derwentwater. And you often see ___________________ jams in the Lake District – not cars but sheep! You can do ________________ of adventure activities like rock ______________________, kayaking, canoeing, ________________________ biking or pony _________________________. We saw the Honister slate ______________, which was fantastic. Years ago they used __________________ and sleds to take the _________________ down the steep paths into the ________________ below. Great Gable is the 7th _________________ mountain in the Lake District. ________________ of people go rock ________________ there."

2 Vocabulary: Odd word out

Find the odd word out.

1	2	3	4	5
path	rowing	wine	soup	starter
valley	windsurfing	beer	pasta	dessert
steak	canoeing	jam	sled	main course
mountain	pony trekking	orange juice	rice	slate
river	kayaking	lemonade	salad	menu
rock	swimming	water	bacon	meal
________	________	________	________	________

3 Vocabulary: Definitions

Write definitions for these words.

1. traffic jam: ______________________________
2. guest: ______________________________
3. slate: ______________________________
4. to book: ______________________________
5. to trek: ______________________________

Ready for the holiday?

1 Grammar: Before the trip

There's a lot to do before the Leinerts can leave for their holiday.
First write what they are doing, and then what they have done.

1. Mr Leinert is shaving in the bathroom.
   Mr Leinert has shaved in the bathroom.
2. ______________________________
   ____
   ____
3. ______________________________
   ____
   ____
4. ______________________________
   ____
   ____
5. ______________________________
   ____
   ____
6. ______________________________
   ____
   ____

2 Grammar: Questions and short answers

Put the verbs in the present perfect und give short answers.

Mr Leinert:

1. Have you packed **(you, pack)** all your things?
2. ______________ **(you, phone)** David?
3. ______________ **(Mum, tidy)** the kitchen?
4. ______________ **(you, wash)** the dishes?
5. ______________ **(Mum, shut)** the windows?
6. ______________ **(you, forget)** your mobile?

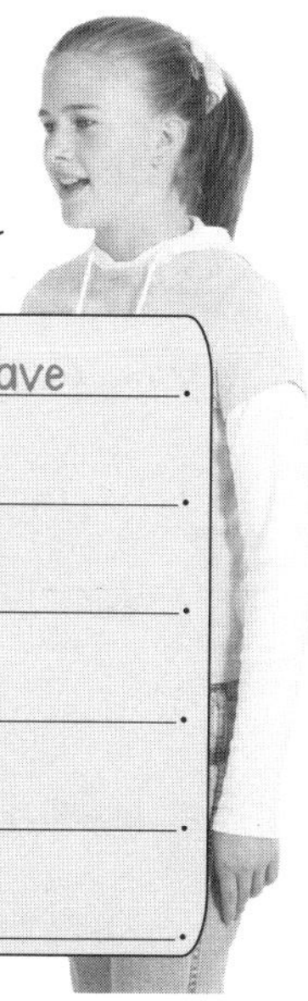

Yes, I have.
No, I ______.
No, she ______.
Yes, I ______.
Yes, she ______.
No, I ______.

3 Grammar: Present perfect

Write down what the Leinerts haven't done yet.

1. Jenny hasn't got up yet. ______________________________
2. Jenny ______________________________
3. Mrs Leinert ______________________________
4. Mr Leinert ______________________________
5. Mrs Leinert ______________________________
6. Mr Leinert ______________________________
7. Jenny ______________________________
8. The Leinerts ______________________________

4 Grammar: Future forms

Put in the right future form.

1. Maybe there ____will be____ **(will be • is going to be)** a good film on TV this evening.
2. ______________ **(will you come • are you going to come)** to my birthday party?" – "No, I can't. But I'm sure you ______________ **(will have • are going to have)** fun."
3. "Can I play with David?" – "I'm sorry, but David ______________ **(will be busy • is going to be busy)** this afternoon. He ______________ **(will clean • is going to clean)** his bike."
4. "What are your plans for tomorrow, David?" – "Robert and I ______________ **(will play • are going to play)** football together."
5. "Have you already made plans for the weekend?" – "Yes, Robert's mum ______________ **(will get • is going to get)** tickets for the match against Arsenal and she ______________ **(will take • is going to take)** us there."

At the Prestons'

1 Mediation: In English, please

Write the dialogue.

1. Herr Preston fragt die Leinerts, ob sie jemals zuvor im Lake District gewesen sind.
   Mr Preston:
2. Herr Leinert antwortet, dass er einmal vor langer Zeit als Student hier gewesen ist.
   Mr Leinert:
3. Frau Preston fragt Frau Leinert, ob sie schon viel herumgefahren sind und was sie bis jetzt gemacht haben.
   Mrs Preston:
4. Frau Leinert bejaht dies und sagt, dass sie schon das meiste des Lake Districts gesehen haben. Sie sind am Sonntag mit dem Auto herumgefahren und haben das gute Wetter ausgenutzt.
   Mrs Leinert:
5. David sagt, dass das Wetter am Sonntag wirklich toll gewesen ist, und dass er viele Fotos gemacht hat.
   David:
6. Frau Leinert sagt, dass sie morgen den Great Gable besteigen und Ausschau nach dem Geist halten werden, besonders wenn es neblig werden wird.
   Mrs Leinert:

2 Grammar: Word order

Make sentences or questions. Put the verbs in the simple past or the present perfect.

1. the Lake District • **(see)** • Mr Leinert • a long time ago
2. **(visit)** • you • yet • the Cumberland Pencil Museum (?)
3. not • David • museum • **(see)** • yet
4. Mrs Preston • 1975 • **(come)** • in (?)

5. their first day • **(travel)** around • the Leinerts • on • in the car

____

6. Mr Leinert • when • for the first time • **(visit)** • the Lake District (?)

____

7. **(meet)** • just • the ghost • the Leinerts

____

8. never • **(be)** • before • David • to the Lakes

____

9. **(buy)** • Jenny • a box • yesterday • Cumberland pencils • of

____

3 Grammar: Simple past or present perfect?

David is in the Lake District. He writes a letter to his friend Mike and tells him about his holiday.
Put in the correct verb forms.

Dear Mike,

We ___arrived___ **(arrive)** here in the Lake District a week ago. The trip ______ **(be)** very exciting so far. ______ you ever ______ **(be)** to this part of Britain? Mr Leinert ______ **(stay)** here a long time ago when he ______ **(be)** young. I ______ never ______ **(see)** this part of Britain. Where ______ you ______ **(spend)** your holidays last summer?

The Leinerts are very nice. They ______ **(show)** me a lot of interesting things so far. I ______ **(meet)** and ______ **(speak)** to some nice people yesterday. Mr Preston, the owner of the bed and breakfast place, ______ **(tell)** us some exciting stories about smugglers and ghosts when we ______ **(stay)** with him at the weekend.

We ______ **(just, come)** back from a boat trip on Ullswater. Yesterday we ______ **(climb)** Great Gable and later in the evening we ______ **(swim)** in the lake, which is very cold, of course. But we all ______ **(enjoy)** it.

The Leinerts ______ **(just, tell)** me to come in for dinner. So I must stop now. That's all for today. See you soon.

Bye, David

Jenny's adventure on Great Gable

1 Cloze test: In the mountains

Fill in the gaps.

Yesterday Mr Preston ______________ the Leinerts to be ______________ out on the mountains. He ______________ his guests because the weather ____________________ in the morning was terrible. Last year there ______________ a bad ______________ up there. After the ______________ got worse and ______________, the path became slippery. It ______________ very difficult to walk. The Leinerts set ______________ in the morning. Later in the afternoon it ____________ to rain and it got wetter and ______________. After some time the Leinerts ________________ voices. They ________________ some young people ______________ were wearing T-shirts. The young man's foot __________________ hurt. He ______________ help immediately. Mr Leinert had his __________________, but he couldn't phone the ____________________ Rescue because his battery didn't ______________. So they left their __________________ and followed the path down ________________ the valley. Suddenly they saw the _________________ of a farm. Mr Leinert knocked at the __________________ and asked the woman: "Please ______________ the Mountain Rescue immediately. A man is ______________ up in the mountains!" The Mountain Rescue people ________________________ the young people.

2 Dictation: Mrs Leinert's postcard to Mrs Penrose

7 Listen to track 7 and write the sentences.

Dear Pat,

____

____

____

____

____

____

____

____

____

____

Helen

3 Mediation: Bad weather

Say it in English. Be careful with the tenses.

1. Gestern ist die Wettervorhersage ziemlich gut gewesen, aber vielleicht wird sich das Wetter heute Nachmittag ändern.

____

____

2. Der Regen hat vor ein paar Stunden begonnen und die Wege sind sehr rutschig geworden.

____

____

3. Wir erinnerten uns an den Unfall, von dem uns Herr Preston erzählt hat, und der letztes Jahr im März oder April geschehen ist.

____

____

____

4 Listening: Barker's holiday in the Lake District

8 Listen to track 8 and answer these questions.
When the answer is 'no', give the right information.

1. Did Barker have bacon and eggs for breakfast?

No, he didn't. He had some dog food for breakfast.

2. Did Barker go for a walk in the hotel?

____

3. Were the other swimmers in the hotel happy with Barker?

____

4. What was Grandpa doing while Grandma was talking about Barker?

____

5. Where is Barker going with Grandpa today?

____

6. Is Grandpa going to paint a picture at Derwentwater?

____

7. Will Barker like swimming in Derwentwater?

____

1 Vocabulary: Crossword puzzle

Across →

1. the months of September, October and November
6. When you want to know what the weather will be like on the next day, you have to listen to the weather …
7. a popular water sport you do with a boat and a paddle (not 'kayaking')
10. to move from one place to another, often as a part of a holiday
11. Obelix fell into a … when he was young.
12. Before you go into a room you … at the door and wait for an answer.

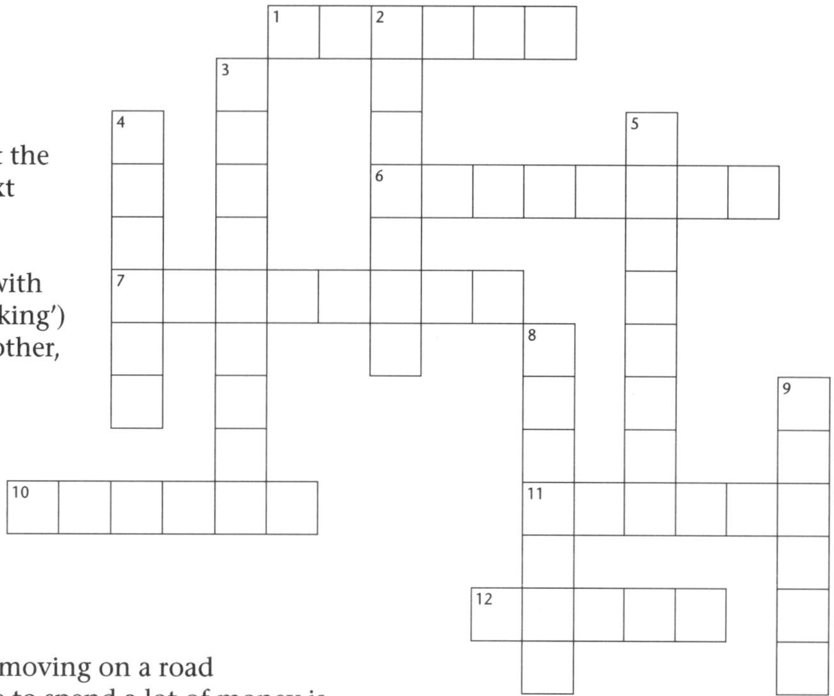

Down ↓

2. all the cars, buses etc. that are moving on a road
3. Something for which you have to spend a lot of money is …
4. help that saves somebody from a dangerous situation
5. The Burtons have two children, Simon is their son and Becky is their …
8. opposite of 'wife'
9. opposite of 'mountain'

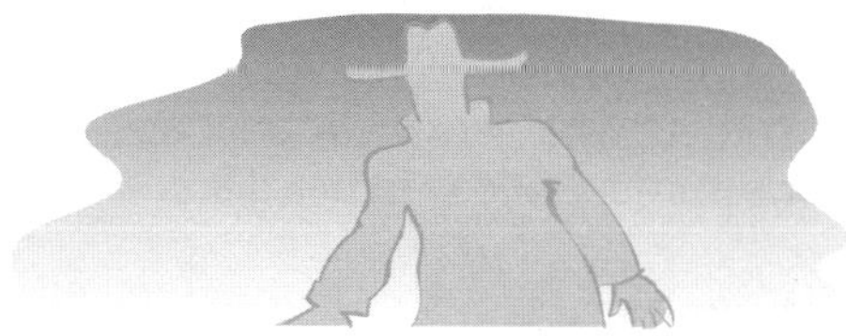

2 Mixed bag: The ghost on Great Gable

Put in the right verb forms.

While the Leinerts ___were looking for___ **(suchen)** help, Jenny ___saw___ **(sehen)** a man in the fog. At first she ________ **(denken)** it was her dad, so she ________ **(folgen)** him. Suddenly the man ________ **(sein)** gone and Jenny's parents ________ **(rufen)** her. Later, when the Leinerts ________ **(ankommen)** at Moses Farm, Jenny ________ **(sprechen)** to Mrs Moses about the man.

Jenny: "________ **(Ihr Mann, arbeiten)** in these mountains?"

Mrs Moses: "No, my husband ________ **(sterben)** a long time ago. Why?"

Jenny: "Oh … sorry. Well, ________ **(Sie, schon, treffen)** a ghost here?"

Mrs Moses: "Yes, I have. Old Moses sometimes ________ **(besuchen)** the farm. He ________ **(leben)** on Great Gable for hundreds of years. ________ **(er, helfen)** you down the mountain?"

Jenny: "Yes, he did! He ________ **(zeigen)** us the right path."

Mrs Moses: "You ________ **(sein)** lucky. Old Moses ________ **(nicht mögen)** people."

revision 2 Unit 3 – Unit 4

1 Grammar: Future forms

Put in the different future forms.

1. Jenny is looking forward to her birthday. Next week she 'll be ________ **(be)** twelve.
   David has got a plan. He ________ **(buy)** her some nice games.
2. David is sure she ________ **(like)** her presents.
3. Jenny hopes she ________ **(get)** a lot of birthday presents.
4. She ________ **(invite)** all her friends to her party. That's her plan.
5. David's parents have just decided: "We ________ **(give)** Jenny a pet!"
6. David hopes they ________ **(buy)** her a dog.
7. Jenny thinks she ________ **(get)** a bike for her birthday.
8. "What are your plans for the party, Jenny?" – "We ________ **(play)** football.
   Maybe the weather ________ **(be)** better."

2 Mixed bag: Jenny's diary

Complete what Jenny wrote about her summer holiday in her diary.

September, 1st

This ________ Mum and Dad ________ to go to the ________. In the morning before ________ left there was chaos at ________ house: We ________ and everything went ________ that morning. When Mum was ________ the ________, Dad ________ the ________ with butter on her foot. Then later, on the road, there was a terrible ________. At the beginning the ________ was ________ and we made the most of ________ and went mountain ________ and pony ________ every day. But when we decided to ________ Great Gable, the weather ________ announced rain and we had to ________ at the hotel. It was ________ outside, really terrible and annoying. No more rock ________, no more ________ adventures, no more ________! We didn't ________ around much because it got ________ and ________. So we stayed in the ________ and watched videos. I really ________ we will have our next ________ in Italy.

At Cooper Middle School

1 Vocabulary: Words and definitions

a) Find the right word.

1. If you work hard at your aims, you will probably have ____________________.
2. If you don't eat enough, you'll get too ________________.
3. Ideas and information that help you to write something are called ____________________.

b) What is it in American English?

1. headmaster	____________________	4. time table	____________________
2. lessons	____________________	5. class or year	____________________
3. programme	____________________	6. flat	____________________

2 Vocabulary: Cooper Middle School

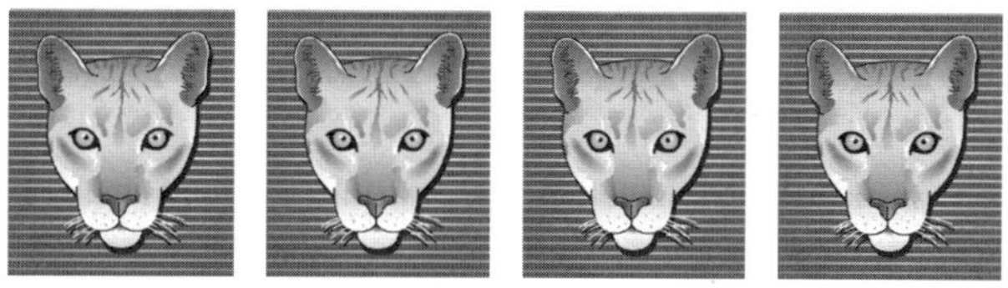

Correct the wrong information.

1. Cooper Middle School is in Haywood.

   Cooper Middle School is in Denver, Colorado.

2. Under 20% of Colorado adults take part in Make A Difference Day.

   ____

3. The 'Mile High City' is at the foot of Dinosaur Ridge.

   ____

4. Denver is the 'green city' because most of the public buildings are green.

   ____

   ____

3 Vocabulary: School activities

Explain what you do in these clubs.

a) Semantics: ____

____

b) Earth Keepers Club: ____

____

c) Drama Club: ____

____

1 Mixed bag: Making plans

Complete the dialogue between Ms Gerlernter and her students with the words and phrases from one of the three boxes. The numbers show you in which box you'll find the answer.

1 German	2 Verbs	3 Phrases
Gemeinde	give	anyway
herumhängen	like	come on
langweilig	look	don't worry
Leute ✔	give	great idea
Müll	not do	how about
nicht wahr?	need	I guess
pflanzen	give	I'm sure
vor	sound	no, thanks
wenigstens	have	wait a minute
Säcke	do	don't know

Ms G: What are you ____guys____ **(1)** going to do on Make A Difference Day?

José: Maybe we could ________ **(1)** some trees ________ **(1)** the school building. If we do that, then the front ________ ________ **(2)** much more interesting.

Ms G: ________ **(3)**. It really looks ________ **(1)** out there. But ________ **(3)** you ________ **(2)** some money for that, ________ **(1)**? ________ **(3)** asking your parents for some? If they ________ **(2)** you some money, I ________ **(2)** you the tools.

Bruce: Hmm! I ________ **(3)**. ________ **(3)**, why don't we just go to Washington Park then and pick up ________ **(1)**?

Tina: Oh, ________ **(3)**, I ________ **(2)** that. That really ________ **(2)** like hard work. ________ **(3)**! Forget it.

José: ________ **(3)**, Tina. Do you just want to ________ **(1)**?

Ms G: Well, ________ **(3)** your parents ________ **(2)** it if you ________ **(2)** something like that for the ________ **(1)**, Tina.

Tina: And what about the ________ **(1)**? We will need ________ **(1)** ten.

Ms G.: ________ **(3)** about that. Mr Weinberger ________ **(2)** you all you need.

Bruce: OK. I think we ________ **(2)** a plan now.

2 Grammar: New in Denver

Use the correct verb form and complete the sentences.

Donna: If I ___go___ **(go)** to CMS next year, I ___'ll join___ **(join)** their girls' soccer team.

Dad: That's a good idea. If you ______ **(do)** that, you ______ **(be)** a superstar in a month.

Donna: Come on, Dad. Don't be silly. But I'm sure that the team ______ **(have)** a lot of success if we all ______ **(work)** together.

Dad: And if you ______ **(not be)** successful, ______ **(you, join)** the Players then?

Donna: The Players? You mean the drama group?

Dad: Yes, they're great. If they ______ **(find)** out how good you are, they ______ **(give)** you a big part in their next school play. And if there ______ **(be)** someone from Hollywood – and sometimes there is – they ______ **(offer)** you a role in a film, and if the film ______ **(become)** a success, you ______ **(be)** a …

Donna: Dad, if you ______ **(say)** that word again, I ______ **(leave)** Denver and never ______ **(come)** back!

3 Writing: Make sentences

Match the parts of the sentences and write them down.

If José and the others pick up trash	I won't answer the phone.
If they ask their parents for help	she won't play in the next game.
When I do my assignment tomorrow morning	they'll need a lot of bags.
When school starts in fall	they'll give them some money.
If Joanne is late for practice	she'll buy some candy.
When Sally goes to the supermarket tomorrow	Donna will be a student at CMS.

1. If José and the others pick up trash, they'll need a lot of bags.
2. ______
3. ______
4. ______
5. ______
6. ______

1 Grammar: When you are grown up ...

What will you ***be allowed to do***, what will you ***have to do*** and what won't you ***have to do*** when you are grown up?

drive a car

go to school

buy your own clothes

work long hours

do homework

go to wild parties

1. When I'm grown up, I'll be allowed to drive a car.
2. ______
3. ______
4. ______
5. ______
6. ______

2 Grammar: Substitute forms

Change the following sentences into a) the past tense and b) the future.

1. The 7th graders can organize a bazaar, but they must ask Ms Gerlernter first.

a) The 7th graders were allowed to organize a bazaar, but they had to ask Ms Gerlernter first.

b) ______

2. Sally and her friends can collect some money for the hospital.

a) ______

b) ______________________________

____

3. Donna needn't do her homework because of her project.

a) ______________________________

____

b) ______________________________

____

4. Sven and Bruce mustn't miss more than two classes on Monday morning.

a) ______________________________

____

b) ______________________________

____

3 Mediation: An e-mail to Sven

Write an e-mail to Sven and get some information about his latest 'Make A Difference Day' project.

1. Begrüße Sven und teile ihm mit, warum du schreibst.
2. Berichte, dass deine Klasse die Erlaubnis hat, ein Projekt mit einem Wohltätigkeitsverein deiner Stadt zu machen.
3. Frage ihn, welches Projekt er und seine Klasse dieses Jahr in Denver gemacht haben, ob die Schüler in seiner Klasse in der Lage gewesen sind, sich auf ein Projekt zu einigen, was sie machen mussten, um genügend Geld zu sammeln und ob er und seine Freunde damit armen Familien in ihrer Gemeinde helfen konnten.

____

____

____

____

____

____

____

____

____

____

____

Donna's diary

1 Vocabulary: Word families

Find a verb or an adjective from the same word family.

1. introduction ___to introduce___
2. difference ______________
3. truth ______________
4. invitation ______________
5. definitions ______________
6. noise ______________
7. fog ______________
8. day ______________
9. winner ______________
10. shot ______________

2 Cloze test: Joanne's story

Fill in the gaps.

Now everybody is angry with ______________. They all think I'm a ______________ jerk or something like that. ______________ all this because I played ______________ little joke on Tina and ______________. Tina really asked for it ______________ she always thinks that she ______________ Miss Wonderful. You know, I ______________ wanted that part in the ______________ play. I thought: If I ______________ this role, I will be ______________ star of the show. But ______________ Tina smiled at Mr Carpeletti ______________ that was it. So she ______________ the part, and what is ______________, her acting was really brilliant. ______________, José is crazy about Tina, ______________, like the rest of the ______________. He has only got eyes ______________ her. I'm not jealous ______________ her, believe me. Maybe I ______________ talk to José about the ______________ and explain to him why ______________ did what I did. I'm ______________ he'll understand.

3 Writing: Donna's diary

In her diary, Donna presents a number of different characters. Bruce Csonka is one of them.
Does he have a reason to hurt Tina and José? And does he have the chance to do so?
Write about 60–70 words to answer these questions.

____

____

____

____

____

____

____

4 Dictation: Acrobats

9 Listen to track 9 and complete the text.

Have you ______________ acrobats ______________ or on TV? What they do is ______________ and takes many ______________. They ______________ with balls or other things ______________ to each other very ______________. Some acrobats throw things ______________, like ______________, or things ______________, like ______________. They can ______________ at the same time, or use their feet to throw and turn things ______________. ______________ their tricks are difficult, ______________ all the time. ______________ you think "______________," but then you see ______________ and ______________ they do.

5 Listening: Make a Difference Day

10 Listen to track 10 and answer the questions.

1. Who was busy while the students were working on their projects?
____
2. Who designed special pages for the website?
____
3. What did Ms Kellermann organize?
____
4. Who took photos of all the students?
____
5. Why was the teachers' play a play with a difference?
____
____
6. Which instrument did Mr Weinberger play in the teachers' band?
____
7. Which stories did Ms Kellermann say she preferred?
____
____
8. Why does José want another Make a Difference Day party?
____
____

1 Mixed bag: José, the mariachi player

Fill in the gaps.

José Fernandez ________________ the trumpet in his dad's mariachi ________________. He has played the trumpet since ____________ was five years old and he has ________________ a fantastic mariachi artist by ________________. One can really say he has ________________ the most of it because in ____________ beginning he had to practice a __________ and sometimes he was quite unhappy ______________ it. Actually, it made him angry ________________ he had to hang around in the house ____________ play the same old songs over and over again ______________ his friends were allowed to ___________ soccer or do something else outside. Sometimes __________ was so bored that he wanted to ______________ his trumpet against the wall. But because his ________________ taught him a feeling of obligation, ___________ finally got past the elementary difficulties ____________ began to enjoy playing his instrument. Now he ____________ imagine a life without his trumpet.

2 Mediation: School rules

Your American penfriend has sent you an e-mail in which he asks you to give him some information about the rules at your school. Write an answer and use these notes.

- Schüler müssen pünktlich zum Unterricht in den Klassenzimmern sein.
- Es ist den Schülern nicht erlaubt, in den Klassenzimmern zu essen. Einige Lehrer erlauben ihnen aber, etwas zu trinken.
- Die Schüler müssen den ganzen Vormittag in der Schule bleiben.
- Und auf dem Schulgelände dürfen sie nicht rauchen (= *to smoke*).

Hi Chris,

Thank you for your e-mail. You wanted to know ________________________________

____

____

____

____

____

____

____

____

____

Focus on travel and transport

1 Vocabulary: Definitions

1. check-in: ______________________________

____

2. boarding pass: ______________________________

____

3. departure: ______________________________

2 Writing: Means of transport

You are in New York City and want to travel to San Francisco on the west coast. Name three possible means of transport and describe the positive and negative points of each. Use if-clauses.

a) I can go by train. If I go by train, ______________________________

____

b) ______________________________

____

c) ______________________________

____

3 Mediation: At SeaTac Airport

You are going to spend a few weeks with your aunt and uncle in Los Angeles. You're at SeaTac Airport in Seattle at the moment and are talking to Aunt Sue on the phone.

1. Teile deiner Tante mit, wo du gerade bist und dass du mit dem Flugzeug nach LA kommen wirst. Die Flugdauer wird etwa drei Stunden betragen und du wirst um 18 Uhr in LA sein.

____

____

____

2. Als deine Tante dich fragt, warum du deine Pläne geändert hast, sagst du, dass du ursprünglich die Strecke von Seattle nach LA mit dem Bus zurücklegen wolltest, dass aber schwere Regenfälle in den Rocky Mountains zu Schwierigkeiten für Busreisende geführt haben.

____

____

3. Du fügst hinzu, dass die Busse von Seattle nach LA mehrere Stunden Verspätung haben und du deshalb denkst, dass das Flugzeug doch der einfachste Weg für die weite Strecke sein wird.

____

____

In the country

1 Mixed bag: The brochure

Put in the missing words.

Visit the Lazy G!

There are many ____________ to come here: The Lazy G is not only a ____________ ranch, it is a real ____________ ranch, too. You will be ____________ to take part ____________ every aspect of ranch life. Branding and ____________ are only two of them. We have got over 600 cows and ____________ on 15,000 acres of land right in the heart of the Rocky ____________ . We can ____________ you a lot of exciting ____________ , for example ____________ riding, camping ____________ or ____________ fishing in one of our clean rivers. If you want to go riding, you need to bring some ____________ : a hat, one or two pairs of jeans, a ____________ jacket and cowboy ____________ . (____________ them in first!) You don't need your own ____________ or chaps and remember that you mustn't use ____________ . Our horses move without them! We are ____________ near Billings where there is an ____________ . Why don't you ____________ us for a week of western fun?

2 Cloze test: A letter

Karen Thompson is a guest at the Lazy G. She writes a letter to her husband. Fill in the gaps.

Dear Steve,

I hope you're fine and you don't ____________ to work too hard. I'm enjoying my ranch ____________ very much. Ed and Martha Gooch are lovely ____________ , the food is simple but delicious and the ____________ are very easy to ride. From my room I ____________ got a beautiful view of the Rocky Mountains. Last ____________ we had a square dance evening. I danced all night, ____________ you needn't be jealous – my partner was an old cowboy. ____________ is seventy-two, but he can dance a lot better ____________ most younger men. I really like country music. Today I ____________ the cowboys on a cattle drive. It was really ____________ . My horse Rusty was the best horse I have ever ____________ . I have just noticed that in another week I'll ____________ to work at the bank again. I hate the idea. ____________ year you will have to try and come, too. Laura would ____________ it here, too. Say hello to my little girl ____________ me. Love to both of you,

Karen

At the Lazy G

1 Grammar: Indefinite pronouns

Ed, Martha, Sally Gooch and Chuck Miller are having dinner at the Lazy G. Put in ***some*** or ***any***.

Martha: You must be hungry. We've got tomato soup tonight. Here's ______________ bread to go with it. Then we have steak and chips …

Ed: Aren't there ______________ potatoes?

Martha: Of course, there are ______________ potatoes for you. I know you don't like chips. Can I go on now?

Ed: Of course, you can. Sorry.

Martha: Well, here's ______________ salad because we haven't got ______________ vegetables today …

Sally: Haven't we got ______________ dessert?

Martha: You're as bad as your uncle, Sally. No, we haven't got ______________ .

Sally/Ed: Oh, no!

Chuck: Don't worry. She's joking. I saw a huge bowl of strawberries in the kitchen.

Sally/Ed: Ah!

Martha: Chuck is right. We're going to have strawberries and cream for dessert. Would you like ______________ ?

Sally/Ed: Of course!

Martha: Okay, but you must wait a little bit. Now, who would like to start with ______________ soup? You, Sally?

Sally: Yes, thank you. But I don't want ______________ bread. I need room for the strawberries.

2 Grammar: What is the right compound?

Put in: every- some- any- no-

1. I can't find my cap. I know I had it when I came home. So it must be ______________where.
2. I can't find my cap. Where can it be? I've looked for it ______________where.
3. I can't find my cap ______________where.
4. Chuck really likes his state, Texas. I think he knows ______________thing about it.
5. Mr Holden thinks people in Montana speak like Chuck. He knows ______________thing about Montana.

3 Grammar: An accident on a cattle drive

some any every no

Put in *some, any, every, no* or their compounds.

Mr Holden: Stop, you stupid horse. Whoa! Help!

Chuck: Don't fall off! Hold on! Oops – too late. Are you OK, Mr Holden?

Mr Holden: No, I'm not OK. I can't see ____________ because there's sand in my eyes. I feel pain[1] ____________ . I think I broke my legs and arms. Isn't ____________ going to help me?

Chuck: Well, I don't think your arms are broken – the way you're waving them about. Let me have a look at your legs. Can you move them? That's good. There's ____________ wrong with you.

Mr Holden: That's what you think. I think I must go to the hospital at once.

Chuck: Let's find out if you can get up first. Can ____________ come and give me a hand? Thanks, Sally. Let's help Mr Holden to get up.

Mr Holden: Oh, that rude[2] girl. I don't want her ____________ near me!

Chuck: Sally is a nice young lady, Mr Holden. She'll help you. That's it, Mr Holden. See? You can stand. ____________ is going to be OK.

Mr Holden: Well, maybe I can stand, but I'm not going to ride that horse any more. He's dangerous.

Sally: He's not! You can't find a better horse ____________ , but you have to treat him right.

Chuck: Easy, Miss Sally. Sorry, Mr Holden, if you don't want to ride Rusty again, choose one of the other horses. You can take ____________ horse you like.

Mr Holden: Then I'll take your horse. But I can tell you one thing. I'm going to spend my next summer vacation ____________ in Florida. No more ranch vacations for me!

[1] [peɪn] – Schmerz • [2] [ru:d] – unverschämt

Mr Holden writes a letter

1 Writing: Make sentences

Match the parts of the sentences and write them down.

Suddenly I realized	trying although it is difficult.
He spoke with	your horse right, you won't have problems.
Keep	forward to our week at the ranch.
When you treat	to the waiter because my omelette didn't come.
We're all looking	that I needed a break.
I had to complain	to be late. He's never on time.
I expected him	a strong accent.

Suddenly I realized that I needed a break.

2 Grammar: Mr Holden's accident

Put in the correct verb forms and be careful with the tenses.

1. If Mr Holden ___goes___ **(go)** to Florida next year, he ___will be able to lie___ **(can, lie)** on the beach all day.
2. Last night Chuck ______ **(must, tell)** Ed Gooch about Mr Holden's accident.
3. Sally ______ **(needn't, worry)** about Rusty because everybody knew that Rusty was a good horse.
4. If a rider ______ **(treat)** Rusty right, he ______ **(have)** a wonderful horse.
5. When Mr Holden came home, he told his friends: "Can you imagine? I ______ **(can't, use)** spurs on that ranch. You can't tell a horse who's boss ______ without them."
6. Chuck rode Rusty the day after Mr Holden's accident and he ______ **(needn't, use)** spurs to tell Rusty what to do.

3 Writing: You want to complain

You're spending your summer vacation in a terrible hotel, although their brochure promised you a wonderful vacation. Complain to the owner of the hotel – he isn't very friendly. Write the dialogue.

That's what the brochure says	That's why you complain
• hotel not far from the beach	• fish and chips every day, no salad
• big swimming pool	• room with a view of the road
• room with a view of the sea	• noisy parties every night
• good food	• must walk 15 minutes to beach
• quiet hotel	• swimming pool very small and not clean

You: I'm not enjoying my summer vacation!

____

____

____

____

Owner: Well, 15 minutes isn't far, an hour is far. And the road is the road to the beach.

Why are you complaining?

You: ______________________________

____

____

Owner: My other guests are enjoying their vacation. That's why they always have parties.

Why don't you go to the parties, too?

You: ______________________________

____

Owner: The fish is good, and the chips are good. A lot of people don't like salad.

You: ______________________________

____

Owner: It's big enough for the children and I think it's clean.

Rusty's story

1 Writing: For and against

Is a vacation in Florida really better than a ranch vacation in Montana? Here are some arguments.
Make notes and put them in the right list. Then write a letter to Mr Holden and tell him what you think.

1. You can relax and lie on the beach in Florida.
2. The weather in Florida is usually better than in Montana, especially in the fall.
3. There are not so many tourists in Montana, so there are no crowds.
4. You learn how people live on a ranch.
5. Summers in Florida can be very hot, so hot that you won't want to leave your hotel room.
6. Some of the activities at a ranch can be dangerous when you come from a city.
7. There are lots of fun activities like swimming, windsurfing, fishing or you can go on a boat trip.
8. The Rocky Mountains are very beautiful.

A vacation in Florida is better than a ranch vacation in Montana.

For	Against
· relax and lie on the beach	· not so many tourists in Montana

Dear Mr Holden,

I have heard that you don't want to spend your vacation on a guest ranch any more. Is it true that you want to go to Florida next summer? In my opinion ______

______ //

In my opinion ______

Yours,

2 Dictation: The guest book

11 Listen to track 11 and write down what Mr Holden wrote in the guest book at the Lazy G.

____

____

____

____

____

____

____

3 Mixed bag: Rodeos

Fill in the gaps.

Many people enjoy going to __________. They think they can see real __________ there and don't realize that they're __________ shows. Of course, it's fun to watch the __________ races. Horse and rider must go as __________ as they can round three colored __________. When a horse knocks a barrel __________, there is a time penalty. The __________ cheer for the best horses and riders. But actually, a __________ of those horses get hurt. You never hear __________ happens to them later.

4 Listening: Welcome to Yellowstone Park

12 Listen to track 12 and finish these statements.

1. You'd love it here. We do great trips __________ __________.
2. If there's somewhere special you would like to see, we can do a special __________ __________ __________ __________ __________.
3. We can also take you for wonderful walks to look for __________ __________ __________ __________.
4. Are you going to take a winter __________ __________ __________?
5. We also have restaurants where the __________ __________ __________ __________.
6. There's such a lot to do in Yellowstone Park every __________ __________ __________ __________.
7. Come and enjoy __________ __________ __________.

1 Vocabulary: Crossword Puzzle

Find the words and put them in.

Across →

2. It's another word for 'mad'.
4. When you don't like people because they are better than you, then you are …
6. You haven't got much room on the left or the right in a … canyon.
8. This is a word for all the animals that don't live in zoos, people's homes or on farms.
9. If you … somebody, you believe that the person is good and won't hurt you.
11. You use them to explain the reasons for your opinion.
14. Is this ring made of … gold or does it only look like it?
15. The … is ringing. The lesson is over now.

Down ↓

1. You are … when you do things others are too frightened to do.
3. It is a word made of two other words, for example some + thing.
5. You wear it over your pullover or sweatshirt. It's shorter than a coat.
7. To say that your opinion is different.
10. This is not a good road. It is so … that I move up and down in my seat when I use it.
12. When you … what a situation is like, you understand why it is like that.
13. I know the words of this song but not the …, so I can't sing it.

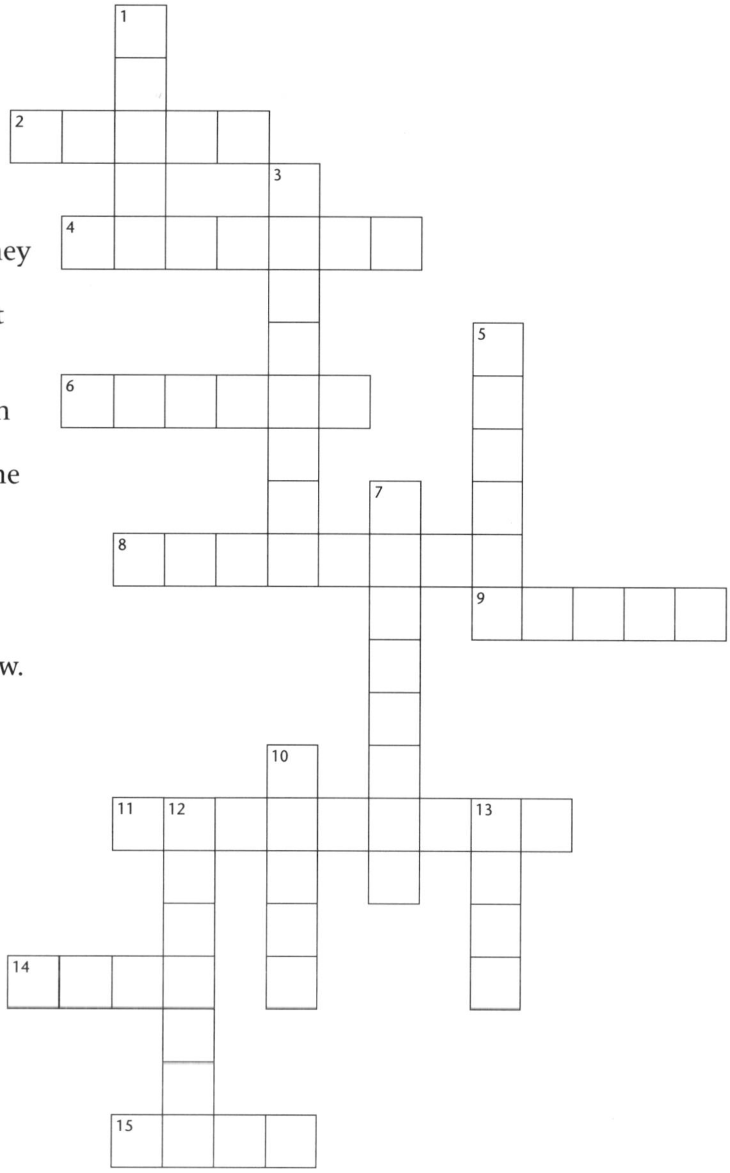

2 Vocabulary: Odd word out

Decide which word is the odd word out and explain in one sentence why you think so.

1	2	3	4	5
budgie	spurs	plain	saucer	nervous
dog	saddle	kitchen	salad	frightened
bear	chaps	mountain	sandwich	excited
cat	laptop	valley	sausage	terrified

1. Bear is the odd word out because a bear is a wild animal (the other animals are pets).
2. ______________________________
3. ______________________________
4. ______________________________
5. ______________________________

Unit 5 – Unit 6

1 Vocabulary: Prepositions

in | of | into | to | over | on

Put in the missing prepositions. You must use some of them more than once.

1. This steak is huge. Divide it ________________ two pieces. You can have one of them.
2. You aren't wearing your glasses. Be careful. Don't knock ________________ that mug.
3. I'll leave your book with our neighbours ________________ case we're out when you come.
4. "What's that noise?" – "Oh, my sister is screaming. She has seen a spider and she is frightened ________________ spiders."
5. Are you looking forward ________________ your ranch vacation?
6. Why are you complaining ________________ me? I didn't tell you to do these exercises.
7. If you don't want to wear these old T-shirts again, get rid ________________ them.
8. Tie your dog ________________ that post over there. You can't take it into the shop.
9. Is the flight ________________ time or is it delayed?
10. Why don't you take part ________________ the project at school?

2 Cloze test: A problem with a calf

Fill in the gaps.

The cows in Montana have a very ________________ life. They're not in a shed, ________________ outside on the plains in the beautiful ________________ Mountains. Their calves can drink their mothers' ________________ and can play with other calves. But ________________ in the mountains can be dangerous, too. ________________ bears or cougars try to kill a calf. ________________ usually can't do it, but they frighten the ________________ and then they run away. That is what ________________ on the day Sally arrived. Chuck rang Martha to ________________ her that a calf was lying in a narrow canyon. ____________ leg was broken. Martha and Ed immediately ________________ to the canyon in their pickup. Ed climbed down to the ________________ and tied a rope round it. He and Chuck ________________ the little animal up. They put it on the ________________ and drove home. Sally phoned the vet. He ________________ after the calf. Chuck brought the calf's ________________ to the ranch. Now they are living in a corral ____________ the calf is OK again.

Heroes and heroines

1 Writing: Who is it?

Explain the link between the two words. Which of the characters on page 84/85 in your textbook is described here? Use the character's name in your sentence.

1. bird • ball

A bird helps Cinderella to go to a ball where a prince falls in love with her.

2. Mississippi • adventures

____

____

3. fight • crime

____

____

4. athletic • archaeology

____

5. Native American chief • English colonist

____

____

6. magic • Lord Voldemort

____

2 Vocabulary: Word puzzle

Find nine (+ two) words that have to do with the heroes and heroines.

1. ______________
2. ______________
3. ______________
4. ______________
5. ______________
6. ______________
7. ______________
8. ______________
9. ______________

C	P	W	I	Z	A	R	D	I	E	R	W
A	R	H	S	A	O	F	S	D	X	Z	A
R	I	U	T	T	I	O	C	E	J	N	R
T	N	W	E	H	U	L	O	N	E	W	C
M	C	G	P	L	M	N	L	T	V	C	H
B	E	B	S	E	C	S	O	I	Q	L	A
P	P	J	I	T	M	H	N	T	K	V	E
Q	L	S	S	I	E	A	I	Y	C	B	O
Y	K	A	T	C	L	I	S	E	R	W	L
M	O	D	E	R	N	V	T	B	F	C	O
X	D	C	R	I	M	E	V	I	L	A	G
C	E	R	S	E	A	C	N	M	P	I	Y

1 Grammar: Adjectives and adverbs

Do you remember this dialogue in your textbook? Fill in the missing adjectives and adverbs. Then underline the adjectives in blue and the adverbs in red.

Bruce: Come in, Donna! Wow, look at you!

You're Lara Croft, right?

Donna: Yes, I am. Who are you?

Bruce: Oh come on, that's an ________________

question to answer. Everyone else recognized me ________________________ enough.

Isn't it ______________________ from the clues? British school uniform. Scar over my eyes.

Donna: Oh, that's a scar. I couldn't see it ____________________ at first. You're Harry Potter!

Bruce: ________________________ girl! And my friend Hermione is somewhere at the party, too.

Donna: Oh yes, there she is. It's Tina. Hey, and there's Otis as Superman. And who's that as Batman?

Bruce: It's José. He's made his costume very ______________________, hasn't he?

But let's go and say hello to Sally – I mean, the Joker. She's standing all alone.

Donna: Hi, Joker. I can see why nobody is talking to you. You're smiling so ______________________!

Sally: Because I *am* ________________. I'm a ________________ guy!

Bruce: Well, please don't behave ________________ at my party.

Sally: OK. It'll be a ________________ job, but I'll try ________________

to be ________________ to everybody.

Bruce: Here's your chance now, Joker. Look, Batman is coming over here.

Sally: Hi, Batman. How are you this evening? What _______________________ ears you have!

Would you like to dance with me? I'm sure you dance __________________________.

José: Huh? What's going on here? Is this the Joker I love to hate?

Donna: He's trying to be ______________________. Say yes, Batman!

Say it ________________________, before he changes his mind!

José: Er – OK. Why not? But don't play any tricks on me while we're dancing, Joker.

Donna: Ha, ha! This is a ________________ party, Bruce. You've organized it really ________________.

Bruce: Come on. Let's dance, too. This is ________________________ ________________________

music – just the thing for ______________________ Lara Croft!

2 Grammar: Adjectives and adverbs

Read what Sally says. While you're reading, underline the adjectives in blue and the adverbs in red. Write them in the right list.

"Donna and I were invited to Bruce's party. I was dressed as Batman and my costume was really cool. Donna was a fantastic Cinderella. Her long dress was really beautiful and everybody recognized her easily. While we were dancing crazily, Donna suddenly screamed loudly. 'There's something under my dress! It's attacking me wildly!' I turned around too quickly to see why Donna was screaming and I fell to the floor with a loud bang. Luckily, I wasn't hurt badly.

Everybody else came to Donna and me excitedly to see what was going on. While I was lying on the floor, I saw the dangerous monster, which was attacking the pretty Cinderella – it was Bruce's cat Susie! The poor thing was so frightened that she ran off fast. Soon we were all laughing merrily because it was such a funny situation. 'You aren't a very realistic Cinderella,' I said to Donna, 'Cinderella isn't afraid of animals, she loves them!'"

Adjectives	Adverbs
cool,	easily,

3 Writing: If I could do magic

What would these characters say if they could do magic? Find the correct word order and make adverbs from the adjectives.

1. *Harry Potter to Lord Voldemort:*

not • world • treat • **(bad)** • the ••• otherwise • fight • I • you • will • **(brave)**

Don't treat the world badly. Otherwise I will fight you bravely.

2. *Cinderella to her stepsisters:*

me • laugh • **(nasty)** • not • at ••• otherwise • you • have to • clean • my shoes • will • **(careful)**

3. *Tom Sawyer to his Aunt Polly:*

not • at • shout • **(angry)** • me ••• otherwise • I • run • **(far)** • will • away

4. *Batman to the Joker:*

smile • not • **(broadly)** ••• have to • you • otherwise • escape • will • **(fast)**

---

5. *Pocahontas to the English colonists:*

people • my • against • fight • not • **(hard)** ••• attack • we • otherwise • you • **(regular)** • will

---

---

6. *Lara Croft to an enemy:*

not • scream • **(loud)** ••• I • into • you • change • can • a • **(easy)** • frog

---

---

4 Grammar: A party

What are these people doing at the party? Use an adverb to describe how they are doing it. The adjectives on the right can help you. What do you think the situation is?

quick • broad • loud • careful • crazy • fast

1. A girl is preparing a salad quickly. Maybe she's a bit late.
2. ______________________________
3. ______________________________
4. ______________________________
5. ______________________________
6. ______________________________

A fun job

1 Grammar: Tina's Uncle Fred

Put in the adverbs.

1. He liked drawing ____________ **(good)** than any other subject. He worked ____________ **(hard)** at Art, harder than at all the other subjects together. He didn't do ____________ **(good)** in some subjects, but in Maths he did ____________ **(bad)** than in the other subjects.
2. He draws important characters ____________ **(careful)** than less important ones and he works ____________ **(careful)** on the hero or heroine, of course! He draws less important characters ____________ **(fast)** than others.
3. Ideas for nasty characters come to him ____________ **(quick)** than for good ones.
4. He likes inventing new characters ____________ **(good)** of all, because he can work ____________ **(free)** and he can draw them as ____________ **(imaginative)** as he likes.

2 Grammar: Comparisons

Make three different comparisons for each picture.

1 run • fast

2 write • imaginative

3 sing • bad

1. Donna runs fastest. She runs ____________ Sally. Sarah doesn't run ____________ Sally and Donna.
2. Alan writes ____________. He writes ____________ José. Bruce doesn't write ____________ José and Alan.
3. Peggy sings ____________. She sings ____________ Sue. Julie doesn't sing ____________ Sue and Peggy.

3 Grammar: Adjective or adverb?

wonderful | fantastic | jealous | good | loud | nice | bad | angry

Normally verbs are followed by adverbs, but some verbs are followed by adjectives. Complete the sentences with the correct form of the words on the right.

1. These flowers smell ________________.
2. Why do you laugh so ________________?
3. Your dress is beautiful. Everybody is looking at you ________________.
4. Are you ill? – Yes, I really feel ________________.
5. Your pizza tastes absolutely ________________.
6. What's wrong? You look ________________.
7. Tina's new boyfriend seems ________________. I really like him.
8. Would you like to come to the cinema with me? – Yes. That sounds ________________.

4 Grammar: How are they doing it?

What are these people doing and how are they doing it? Use a different adverb in each sentence.

1. Tom and Huck are watching the gangsters nervously.
2. ________________
3. ________________
4. ________________
5. ________________
6. ________________

The Native American Cinderella

1 Dictation: A costume for a party

13 Listen to track 13 and complete the text.

You can ______________________ a costume for a party, but ______________________: it must be ______________________.

If your costume is ______________________ or ______________________ you ______________________ the party.

And think: ______________________ in your costume?

Can you __________, ______________________ in it?

If you don't want people to ______________________, then you will ______________________ a mask. ______________________, your friends will ______________________ from the way you ______________________.

You can be ______________________, a book or a fairy story.

Or you can be ______________________ and make a ______________________ of a ______________________. The only thing ______________________ is ______________________.

2 Listening: A quiz about film characters

14 Listen to track 14. Then put the words in the right order and make sentences.

1. nasty • are • frogs • green • and

   Frogs ______________________

2. time • the • all • and • broadly • smiles • is • he • black • white • and

   He ______________________

3. man • world • character • is • this • the • in • strongest • the

   This ______________________

4. magic • learns • he • school • he • student • is • where • a • at • a

   He ______________________

5. nasty • about • green • angry • something • becomes • and • he • when • feels • he

   When ______________________

   ____

focus 4
Focus on traditions

1 Vocabulary: Definitions

Complete the definitions.

1. A ____________________ person likes playing tricks on other people.
2. A ____________________ is another word for Indian.
3. A __________ uses __________ to do fantastic things that other people can't do.
4. A ________________ is a story which isn't true.
5. In a ________________ you find many books.
6. ________________ is another word for film.

2 Cloze test: Traditions

Fill in the gaps.

Four young people are talking about the ____________ differences between their families' countries.

José: In our family ____________ are very important. Mexican people don't only speak English, __________ speak Spanish, too. We also play traditional music __________ typical instruments in my dad's mariachi band. For the ____________, my mum made me a real charro, our special ____________.

Tina: My family is Danish, but I don't know ____________ about Denmark, the country of my great-great-grandparents. What I do ____________ is that people there have big parties or ________________ for special events, e. g. the 50th wedding anniversary of ________ grandparents. We had so many wonderful cakes and __________ asked my grandma to give me some ____________ because I wanted to try them at home and ____________ know how to make them.

Donna: I'm from an Asian ______________ and my parents have a restaurant because they ____________ to cook the traditional food of their home ____________. And their restaurant is always decorated with beautiful ____________.

John: For a long time we weren't allowed to ______________ our traditions. But now one ________ the biggest Native American events is the Crow __________ in Montana, where you can see rodeos and ________________ with many people in colorful costumes, who move ____________ the streets to celebrate.

GREEN LINE NEW 2

Bayern

LEARNING ENGLISH

Lösungsheft zum
Trainingsbuch
Schulaufgaben

Klett

LEARNING ENGLISH **GREEN LINE NEW 2**
Ausgabe für Bayern

Lösungsheft zum Trainingsbuch Schulaufgaben

von
Robert Bauer, Nürnberg; Raimund A. Mader M. A., Eschenbach i. d. Oberpfalz; Peter Müller, Herzogenaurach; Mechthild Murau, Burgthann; Renate Leive, Sonnefeld; Sabine Scherer, Hummeltal; Anja Schmidt, Höchberg

sowie
Faith Puleston, Wetter; Jennifer Wood B. A., Bristol

Illustrationen
Dorothee Wolters, Köln; Elsie Lennox, London

Zeichenerklärung

1 Übungen mit diesem Symbol verweisen auf die hinten im Trainingsbuch eingeklebte CD. Die Ziffer kennzeichnet die Tracknummer. Die Hörtexte sind nicht abgedruckt.

Bildquellenverzeichnis
Umschlag: (1) Getty Images/Reese, Stone; (2) Getty Images/PhotoDisc; (3) IFA/Heron; (4) ZEFA/Studio Wartenberg; S. 3: Ernst Klett Verlag/Smith; S. 6: Ernst Klett Verlag/Smith; S. 22: (1–4) Ernst Klett Verlag/Smith; S. 31: Ernst Klett Verlag/Smith; S. 61: Corbis/Kirkland; S. 64: (1) Robert Harding Picture Library Ltd./; (2) Corbis GmbH; (3) Corbis GmbH/Lewine; (4) Mauritius/Weyer

Copyrightangaben zur CD
Aufnahmeleitung: Ernst Klett Verlag
Regie: Andrew Branch für RBA Productions
Sprecherinnen und Sprecher: Sophie Aldred, Jenny Bryce, Tyler Butterworth, Jordan Calvert, Jimmy Chamberlain, Hollie Chapman, James Daley, DeNica Fairman, Rupert Farley, John Foley, Jenny Funnell, Teresa Gallagher, James Goode, Nigel Greaves, John Hasler, Camilla Hunsley, Hugh Kermode, Walter Lewis, Eric Meyers, Rhonda Millar, Liza Ross, Dominic Rowntree, Amber Rose Sealey, Susan Sheridan, Adam Sims, Zoe Thorne, Patience Tomlinson, Steven Webb, Jane Whittenshaw, Jo Wyatt
Tontechnik: Mark Smith at Air-Edel Studios, London;
Schnitt und Mischung: Andrew Branch und Air-Edel Studios, London
Presswerk: P+O Compact-Disc GmbH, Diepholz.

1. Auflage

1 10 | 2010

Internetadresse: http://www.klett.de

Redaktion: Heinz-Peter Gerlinger (Projektleitung),
Gaby Bauer-Negenborn (Außenredaktion)
Gestaltung: Marietta Heymann

Umschlaggestaltung: Christian Dekelver, Weinstadt
Reproduktion: Meyle + Müller, Medienmanagement, Pforzheim
Druck: Bercker, Kevelaer
ISBN-13: 3-12-547271-6
ISBN-10: 3-12-547271-7

9 783125 472716

Back to school

1 Grammar: Simple past

Put the verbs in the simple past.

David *had* (have) a lot of fun in the holidays. He *went* (go) to New York with his parents and *visited* (visit) his aunt and his cousin. Aunt Meg *met* (meet) them at the airport and *drove* (drive) them to her apartment. After dinner David and Mary-Beth *played* (play) computer games. On their second day Aunt Meg *showed* (show) them the skyscrapers of Manhattan and they *stood* (stand) on the roof of the Empire State Building. In the evening they *watched* (watch) an American football game. Two of Mary-Beth's friends *came* (come) with them. After the game the children *talked* (talk) about the teams and David's new friends *told* (tell) him a lot of interesting things about American football. They *didn't go* (not go) to a baseball game because the team *wasn't* (not be) in New York that week. David *bought* (buy) some souvenirs of New York and *took* (take) lots of photos. He *wrote* (write) postcards to his friends in England, but he only *sent* (send) some of them. He *carried* (carry) the postcard to his best friend Robert in his pocket until the end of the trip! When they *were* (be) back home in Nottingham, David *gave* (give) Robert the postcard and they both *laughed* (laugh). The other children *got* (get) their postcards two days later!

2 Vocabulary: Profile

Put in the missing words.

Name: Glen Parker
Age: 12
Nationality: British
Address: 22 Court Road, London
Hobbies: Football, computers
Likes: Leeds United, chocolate
Dislikes: Bullies, fish and chips
Favourite band / pop star: Robbie Williams
Brothers and sisters: One sister (Kate), 10

Activities at Haywood

1 Grammar: Going-to future

Put the verbs in the going-to future.

1. Becky *is going to play* (play) table tennis with Carina.
2. The two girls *are going to meet* (meet) for a game every Monday.
3. Scott *is going to come* (come), too.
4. Carina *isn't going to join* (not join) the drama group.
5. *Carina:* "Scott, *are* you *going to sing* (sing) in front of the others?"
6. *Scott:* "Well, I *'m* not *going to sing* (sing) but I *'m going to dance* (dance)."
7. Becky *is* not *going to take* (take) Barker to the pet club.
8. The children *are going to talk* (talk) about pets, and they *are going to take* (take) photographs of them.
9. *David:* "Carina, *are* you *going to join* (join) the pet club, too?"
   Carina: "No, I *'m not*. I'm allergic to cats."
10. Robert *is going to go* (go) to the basketball club meeting.
11. Scott and David *are going to look* (look) for old clothes for the second-hand shop.

2 Grammar: Plans for the weekend

Look at the pictures and write down what the people are going to do at the weekend.

buy | go shopping | clean | watch | call

1. Robert *is going to buy a football*.
2. Becky and Sarah *are going to go shopping*.
3. Mr Burton *is going to clean the floor*.
4. *Mark:* "I *'m going to watch TV*."
5. *Becky:* "Carina, *are you going to call your mum*?"
   Carina: "Yes, *I am*."

3 Speaking: A new boy at Haywood School

Put in the question tags. Give short answers and correct the wrong statements.

1. Nice weather today, *isn't it*? Yes, *it is*.
2. You're new here, *aren't you*? Yes, *I am*.
3. Your name is David, *isn't it*? No, *it isn't*. *It's* Scott.
4. You're not American, *are you*? Yes, *I am*.
5. Americans like fast food, *don't they*? Well, most Americans *do*. But I *don't*.
6. But you can play basketball, *can't you*? Yes, *I can*, but I'm not very good.
7. You live in Sherwood, *don't you*? Yes, *I do*.
8. Your dad works here, *doesn't he*? Yes, *he does*.
9. You've got a brother, *haven't you*? No, *I haven't*. *I've got* a sister.
10. You came here by plane, *didn't you*? Yes, of course *I did*!
11. You were here last year, *weren't you*? No, *I wasn't*!
12. You don't talk much, *do you*? Well, not always. But sometimes I *do*.
13. You're not angry, *are you*? Well, … not really.
14. But you'd like to go now, *wouldn't you*? Yes, *I would*. Bye!

4 Mediation: At a British school

Stell dir vor, du bist zu Besuch an einer englischen Schule. Was sagst du auf Englisch, wenn …

1. … dir gerade jemand vorgestellt worden ist?
Nice to meet you!
2. … du meinst, dass viel los ist an dieser Schule?
There's a lot going on at this school.
3. … du etwas schade findest?
What a pity!
4. … du jemanden wissen lassen willst, dass du leider nicht einer Meinung mit ihm / ihr bist?
Sorry, but I don't agree.
5. … du jemanden fragen willst, warum er / sie sich nicht der Theatergruppe anschließt?
Why aren't you going to join the drama club?
6. … du jemanden fragen willst, ob er / sie etwas sucht?
Are you looking for something?
7. … du jemandem mitteilen willst, dass du niesen musst, wenn eine Katze in deiner Nähe ist?
Cats make me sneeze!

Drama at the drama club

1 Grammar: Past progressive

On Sunday Becky took Barker for a walk in the park.
What was happening when Becky and Barker arrived at the park?

1. Two girls *were dancing*.
2. A girl *was reading* a book.
3. A boy *was riding* his bike.
4. Two girls *were playing* football.
5. A woman *was sitting* under a tree.
6. A boy *was lying* in the grass[1].
7. A man *was eating* an ice cream.
8. Two dogs *were chasing* a cat.

[1] [gra:s] – Gras

2 Grammar: Simple past or past progressive?

Put the verbs in the correct tense.

Yesterday Robert and David *were playing* (play) football when it *started* (start) to rain. While they *were walking* (walk) home, the rain *stopped* (stop), but they *didn't want* (not want) to stay outside. When they *arrived* (arrive) at the Penroses' house, Mark *was sitting* (sit) in the living room. He *was watching* (watch) TV. David *said* (say) to him: "Please go to your room, Mark!" But Mark *didn't answer* (not answer). So David *tried* (try) it again: "Hey, Mark, didn't you hear what I said?" But Mark *stayed* (stay) where he *was* (be). This *made* (make) David really angry, but then Robert *had* (have) an idea: "Let's play your new computer game!" – "Great idea!"

3 Mediation: What a great show!

Write down what happened in the drama club.

1. Viele Leute schauten zu, als die Kinder in der Theatergruppe zeigten, was sie können.

A lot of people were watching while the kids in the drama club were showing what they could do.

2. Aber alles ging schief!

But everything went wrong!

3. Ein Mädchen stolperte über das Bein ihres Partners, während sie tanzten.

A girl tripped over her partner's leg while they were dancing.

4. Ein anderes Mädchen sang gerade ein Lied, als jemand von seinem Stuhl fiel.

Another girl was singing a song when somebody fell off his chair.

5. Also hörte sie auf, weil alle lachten.

So she stopped because everybody was laughing.

6. Während ein Junge einen Witz erzählte, warf er sein Handy einem anderen Jungen zu.

While a boy was telling a joke, he threw his mobile to another boy.

7. Aber der andere Junge fing es nicht – er ließ es fallen!

But the other boy didn't catch it – he dropped it!

4 Vocabulary: Prepositions

Put in the right prepositions.

1. Do you do your homework __in__ the afternoon?
2. In the holidays we were __at__ the seaside.
3. Sarah and Becky showed Carina __around__ their school.
4. Wayne and Barry fell __off__ their skateboard.
5. The skateboard flew __across__ the stage.
6. I talked to him __on__ the telephone.
7. My birthday is __on__ March 17th.
8. Let's meet __at__ lunchtime!

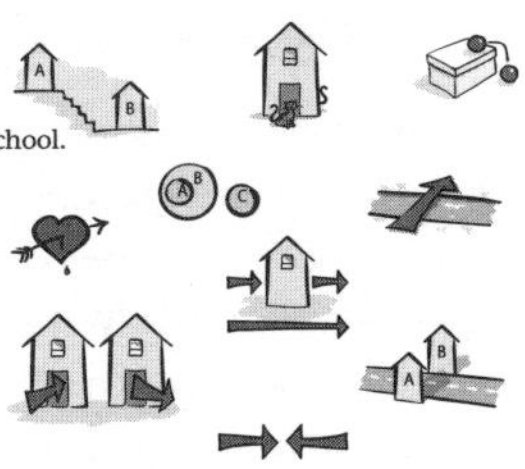

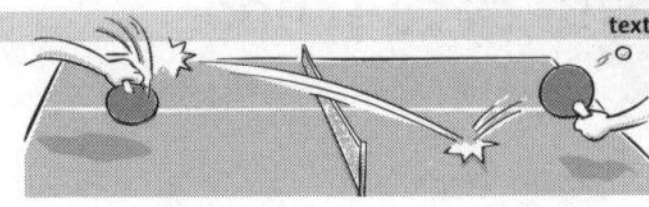

1 Cloze test: A bully

Fill in the gaps.

When Carina plays table tennis __against__ her brother, she sometimes wins and sometimes __loses__. At Haywood the kids can play at the __activity__ centre. While Carina and Becky __were__ playing there in the lunch __break__ last Monday, Wayne and his nasty __gang__ came in. "Girls, it's our __turn__ now," said Wayne and __grabbed__ the bat from Becky. Carina __wanted / tried__ to help her friend, but Barry __pushed__ her away. Then the boys got __ready__ to play. "We don't want any __trouble__ with them," said Becky. "Wayne __thinks__ it's his table because __he__ is in the school table tennis __team__." Carina was watching Wayne and Barry __while__ they were playing. Wayne sometimes __hit__ the ball so hard that Barry __missed__ it. Then Carina went back __to__ the table. "You're not __holding__ the racket right, boy!" she __told__ Wayne. "Racket? This is a bat! __Don't__ girls know anything about sport?"

2 Writing: A great game

Match the parts of the sentences and write them down.

1. Carina grabbed Barry's bat	but	Carina made a joke.
2. Wayne ran,	because	they wanted to watch.
3. The other kids stopped their games	while	she won the game.
4. I missed the ball	when	they weren't good enough.
5. Everybody laughed	so	people were making so much noise.
6. Wayne tried a lot of tricks,	but	he was waiting for Wayne's return.
7. Carina was too good for Wayne,	because	the ball was too fast for him.

1. Carina grabbed Barry's bat while he was waiting for Wayne's return.
2. Wayne ran, but the ball was too fast for him.
3. The other kids stopped their games because they wanted to watch.
4. I missed the ball because people were making so much noise.
5. Everybody laughed when Carina made a joke.
6. Wayne tried a lot of tricks, but they weren't good enough.
7. Carina was too good for Wayne, so she won the game.

3 Grammar: Word order

Put the verbs in the simple past or the past progressive and use *when* or *while*.

1. Becky • a • **(run)** • the • she • CD • park • **(listen to)** • in

Becky was listening to a CD while she was running in the park.

2. Scott • **(meet)** • school • he • home • **(walk)** • Wayne • from

Scott was walking home from school when he met Wayne.

3. Sarah • mobile • her • **(do)** • her • Jenny • **(call)** • homework • on • her

Sarah was doing her homework when Jenny called her on her mobile.

4. Robert • his • **(fall)** • he • arm • **(break)** • bike • off • his

Robert broke his arm when he fell off his bike.

5. David • noise • a • **(read)** • a • **(hear)** • book • he

While David was reading a book, he heard a noise.

6. Mark • in • room • **(play)** • his • **(watch)** • parents • TV • his

Mark was playing in his room while his parents were watching TV.

4 Dictation: Carina is from Bavaria

1 Listen to track 1 and write the sentences.

Carina comes from Germany, but she's in Nottingham now. Her favourite school subject is PE and she likes English, too. In her free time she reads and draws. She is twelve years old and has got two brothers. Her little brother is nine years old; her big brother is 16. He is very good at table tennis. He is a champion player in Bavaria. When she is at home, Carina plays table tennis with him. Usually she loses, but sometimes she wins.

1 Vocabulary: Useful phrases

Put in the missing words.

1. "You are Becky, __aren't you__?" – "__Actually__, I'm Sarah."
2. "How are you?" – "__Fine__, thanks. And you?"
3. "__Would__ you like something to drink?" – "Yes, please."
4. "Can I use your mobile, please?" – "Yes, of course. __Here__ you are."
5. "Atishoo!" – "__Bless__ you!"
6. "I'm in year 8." – "__Me__ too."
7. "We wear school uniform." – "Really? __What's__ it like? Is it nice?"
8. "Did you __have__ a good holiday?" – "No, I didn't! It was terrible."

2 Speaking: Question tags

Say it in English and use question tags.

1. Du interessierst dich für Basketball, nicht wahr?

You're interested in basketball, aren't you?

2. Sarah ist nicht der Theatergruppe beigetreten, oder?

Sarah didn't join the drama club, did she?

3. Carina ist zu Besuch an unserer Schule, stimmt's?

Carina is visiting our school, isn't she?

4. Scott hat ein tolles Skateboard, nicht wahr?

Scott has got a great skateboard, hasn't he?

5. Wir können mittags Tischtennis spielen, oder?

We can play table tennis at lunchtime, can't we?

3 Grammar: Simple past or past progressive?

Put in the correct verb forms.

Yesterday Sarah __was riding__ **(ride)** her bike when she __saw__ **(see)** Scott. He __was talking__ **(talk)** to another boy. "Hello Scott!" Sarah __said__ **(say)**, but Scott __didn't hear__ **(not hear)** her because he __was shouting__ **(shout)** at the other boy. Sarah __got__ **(get)** off her bike and __went__ **(go)** over to the two boys. When Scott __saw__ **(see)** her, he __stopped__ **(stop)** shouting. While Scott __was telling__ **(tell)** Sarah why he was so angry, the other boy __was watching__ **(watch)** them. Suddenly he __ran__ **(run)** away.

1 Writing: Tips for trick-or-treating

Fill in the missing words and match the parts of the sentences.

1. Always go in ___groups___ — b) and take an ___adult___ with you.
2. Never go into ___strangers'___ houses
3. ___Look___ right and left
4. Explain how you want to ___use___ the money
5. ___Be___ friendly and thank everybody

a) to ___help___ other people.
b) and take an ___adult___ with you.
c) when they give you money or ___sweets___ .
d) because you don't ___know___ what's inside.
e) before you go ___across___ the street.

2 Writing: The history of Halloween

Write two short texts about the history of Halloween. Use the given words and think of good verbs.

1. Celtic • Ireland • end of summer • October 31st • scary • ghosts

The Celtic people of Ireland celebrated the end of summer on October 31st.

They wore scary costumes to chase away ghosts.

2. Christians • village • November 2nd • soul cakes • prayer

Christians walked from village to village on November 2nd and asked for soul cakes.

When somebody gave them a soul cake, they said a prayer.

3 Listening: The end of Grandpa's ghost story?

2 Listen to track 2 and complete the sentences.

The barn went ___cold___ ___and___ ___quiet___ .

Our masks were lying ___on___ ___the___ ___floor___ .

We're going to wait for the ghost to ___walk___ ___through___ ___this___ wall here. Somebody was ___walking___ ___around___ the barn. Suddenly, somebody in a red mask came into ___the___ ___light___ ___from___ the lantern. It was the farmer, and he ___was___ ___very___ ___angry___ . Next day I went back to the field, and the barn ___was___ ___empty___ .

1 Vocabulary: Crossword

Across →

4. A lot of people have tea or ... for breakfast.
6. Singers need it on stage, so that people can hear them.
8. If you can't ... what a country is like, you must go and see it. If you can't ... what a person is like, you must meet him or her.
10. The number, the street and the place where you live.
12. Opposite of 'child'.

Down ↓

1. What a lot of people do on their birthday.
2. A huge vegetable. People put a light in it on Halloween.
3. "Why don't you ... our tennis club? Then we can play tennis together every week."
5. People in church usually sing and say ... together.
7. Another word for 'to get (lunch, breakfast etc.) ready'.
9. Opposite of 'nice' (when you speak about a person).
11. To bring the ball into play (at tennis or table tennis).

2 Grammar: Simple form or progressive form?

Every morning Sarah ___gets___ **(get)** up at six o'clock. But not yesterday. Yesterday she ___was___ **(be)** late. When the alarm clock ___woke___ **(wake)** her up for the second time, she ___was still lying___ **(still, lie)** in bed. But then she ___jumped___ **(jump)** out of bed and ___ran___ **(run)** into the bathroom and afterwards she ___hurried___ **(hurry)** into the kitchen. While she ___was standing___ **(stand)** at the bus stop, she ___saw___ **(see)** Becky in a car. Her father ___was driving___ **(drive)** her to school. They ___stopped___ **(stop)**.

Sarah: "I have missed my bus. Now I ___'m___ **(be)** late."

Becky: "___Don't worry___ **(not worry)**. We ___can take___ **(can, take)** you to school in our car."

1 Grammar: Comparisons

Make three different comparisons for each picture.

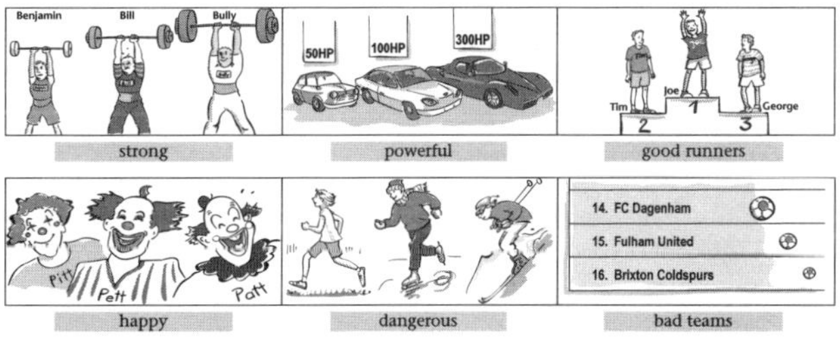

1. Bill is stronger than Benjamin, but he is not as strong as Bully. Bully is the strongest of the three.
2. The Mercedes is ___more powerful than___ the Mini, but it isn't ___as powerful as___ the Ferrari. The Ferrari is ___the most powerful___ of the three.
3. Tim is ___a better runner than___ George, but he isn't ___as fast / good as___ Joe. Joe is ___the best runner___ of the three.
4. *Pett is happier than Pitt, but he isn't as happy as Patt.*
   Patt is the happiest of the three.
5. *Skating is more dangerous than jogging, but it isn't as dangerous as skiing.*
   Skiing is the most dangerous sport of the three.
6. *Fulham United is worse than FC Dagenham, but it isn't as bad as Brixton Coldspurs.*
   Brixton Coldspurs is the worst team of the three.

2 Grammar: Texas is best!

Bud, a boy from Texas, visits David in Nottingham. They go to the Sherwood Forest Visitor Centre together with David's friend Paul. Bud thinks that everything is better in Texas. Fill in the correct form of the adjective.

tip

=	Gleichheit
+	Komparativ (Ungleichheit)
–	Komparativ (Ungleichheit, verneint)
++	Superlativ

Paul: Where in Texas are you from, Bud?

Bud: I'm from Dallas, the **(beautiful ++)** ___most beautiful___ city in the USA. It has also got the **(busy ++)** ___busiest___ airport in the world.

Paul: But I think New York has **(good +)** ___better___ and also **(high +)** ___higher___ skyscrapers than Dallas. And Dallas is **(big –)** ___not as big as___ New York. New York is a much ___more exciting___ **(exciting +)** city.

Bud: I'm sure people in New York are **(friendly –)** ___not as friendly as___ people in Texas. They also drive a lot **(bad +)** ___worse than___ Texans and their cars are much **(small +)** ___smaller than___ our cars.

Paul: Oh, come on! For you cars are **(important +)** ___more important than___ anything else. I think cars are **(boring ++)** ___the most boring___ thing in the world.

David: Your hobby is planes. I think cars are just **(interesting =)** ___as interesting as___ planes. But let's watch that film about Robin Hood now, England's **(famous ++)** ___most famous___ folk hero. He still is **(popular +)** ___more popular than___ anybody else here in England.

3 Mediation: In English, please

1. Die sächsischen Kleinbauern waren ärmer als die meisten Normannen.
   The Saxon peasants were poorer than most of the Normans.
2. Jeder weiß, dass Robin Hood schlauer als der Sheriff von Nottingham war.
   Everyone knows that Robin Hood was cleverer than the Sheriff of Nottingham.
3. Er ist immer noch der berühmteste Volksheld in England.
   He still is the most famous folk hero in England.
4. Für England ist er genau so wichtig wie Wilhelm Tell für die Schweiz (= *Switzerland*).
   For England he's just as important as Wilhelm Tell for Switzerland.
5. Heute ist das Leben in Nottingham nicht ganz so aufregend wie im Mittelalter.
   Today life in Nottingham isn't as exciting as in the Middle Ages.
6. Aber Nottingham wird immer beliebter bei (= *with*) Touristen.
   But Nottingham is getting more and more popular with tourists.

A play

1 Grammar: About sports

Write about the different people in the pictures. Make sentences with *who* or *whose*.
Start with *There is ... / There are ...*

1. There are a boy and a girl whose hobby is football.
2. There are some girls ***who are good at hockey.***
3. There is ***a girl whose brother collects posters of basketball stars.***
4. ***There is a woman whose neighbour's favourite sport is golf.***
5. ***There are two boys who often play basketball in front of their house.***
6. ***There are some young people who think skiing in the mountains is great fun.***
7. ***There is a man whose children like swimming competitions.***
8. ***There is a man whose motto is 'no sports'.***

2 Mediation: A pop concert

Stephanie went to a pop concert last week. She wants to tell her English friend what happened there.

1. Das Konzert, auf das ich letzte Woche ging, war toll.

The concert (that / which) I went to last week was great.

2. Viele Leute, die ich dort traf, kamen von weit her.

Many people (that / who) I met there came from far away.

3. Ein Mädchen, mit dem ich einige Zeit sprach, kam aus Deutschland.

One girl (that / who) I talked to for some time came from Germany.

4. Ich mochte die Lieder, die die irische Gruppe sang.

I liked the songs (that / which) the Irish group sang.

5. Die Fotos, die meine Freundin machte, waren schrecklich.

The photos (that / which) my friend took were terrible.

6. Hier sind die Fotos, die ich von dem Konzert in der Zeitung gefunden habe.

Here are the photos of the concert (that / which) I found in the newspaper.

7. Die Eintrittskarte, die mir meine Eltern zum Geburtstag kauften, kostete 15 Pfund.

The ticket (that / which) my parents bought for my birthday was 15 pounds.

3 Grammar: Contact clause

Lewis is visiting Nottingham and sends texts from his mobile to his friends. He uses contact clauses in all his sentences. Start with the underlined words.

THEY HAVE A FANTASTIC FOREST HERE.

YOU CAN SEE A HUGE OLD OAK IN THIS FOREST.

WE WENT TO A MOST INTERESTING VISITOR CENTRE.

I TRIED OUT A REALLY GREAT HISTORIC LONGBOW.

THEY SELL INTERESTING SOUVENIRS OF NOTTINGHAM THERE.

THEY SHOW A QUITE BORING VIDEO ON KING JOHN.

YOU CAN BUY NICE POSTERS OF ROBIN HOOD THERE.

BUT SOMEONE MADE A VERY STUPID JOKE ABOUT MY BASEBALL CAP[1].

1. The forest they have here is fantastic.
2. The old oak ***you can see in the forest is huge.***
3. ***The visitor centre we went to was most interesting.***
4. ***The historic longbow I tried out was really great.***
5. ***The souvenirs of Nottingham they sell there are interesting.***
6. ***The video they show on King John was quite boring.***
7. ***The posters of Robin Hood you can buy there are nice.***
8. ***But the joke someone made about my baseball cap was very stupid.***

[1] [kæp] – Kappe, Mütze

Robin Hood and the silver arrow

1 Speaking: Looking at photos

Sarah and Pat are looking at the photos of their trip to London. Use contact clauses.

Sarah: the boy (we / meet / station)
Pat: the girl (we / see / zoo)
Sarah: the man (we / talk to / Trafalgar Square)
Pat: the people (Betty / ask for the way)
Sarah: the statue (Sandra / take a photo of / near Big Ben)
Pat: the two guides (some tourists / joke about / the Tower / because they were so funny)

Sarah: Look, this is the boy we met ***at the station.***

Pat: ***And this is the girl we saw at the zoo.***

Sarah: ***That's the man we were talking to at Trafalgar Square.***

Pat: ***And these are the people Betty asked for the way.***

Sarah: ***This is the statue Sandra took a photo of near Big Ben.***

Pat: ***And those are the two guides some tourists were joking about at the Tower because they were so funny.***

2 Dictation: Haywood School Drama Group

3 Listen to track 3 and complete the text.

Haywood School has a ***very good*** drama group. Sometimes the boys and girls in the group find a play ***that they like*** and act it. But ***they often write*** plays, too. They find a ***good story*** with ***interesting characters*** and write the dialogues for them. Sometimes they are very ***clever*** and ***invent exciting scenes***.

Then they ***choose*** the ***right*** people ***for the parts***.

In some of their plays they need lots of people ***who can act***. Some people in the drama group don't want ***a role*** in every play, but ***they help*** with the stage ***and the costumes***.

One year there was a Schools' Drama ***Festival*** with ***a competition***.

The Haywood drama group ***didn't win*** it, but they ***won the first round*** and they were ***in the final***. The drama group plays are ***usually*** very ***popular*** and ***crowds*** of people go to watch them.

3 Vocabulary: Words in disguise

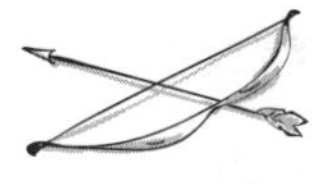

Find ten words that have to do with Robin Hood's favourite sport. Mark them and write them down in alphabetical order.

w	e	a	t	h	c	r	o	w	d	c	k
x	c	f	g	h	l	v	h	i	m	p	f
h	d	s	a	n	r	o	u	n	d	h	n
g	x	p	r	f	g	h	l	n	s	x	t
h	f	d	c	r	e	s	s	e	d	s	a
m	i	x	h	o	b	t	a	r	g	e	t
j	n	e	e	d	o	a	c	r	j	g	f
u	a	r	r	o	w	h	y	p	s	o	l
d	l	o	y	v	o	c	x	y	h	s	d
u	w	i	n	d	k	g	b	o	o	t	f
s	c	o	m	p	e	t	i	t	o	r	i
e	f	n	s	u	n	s	c	r	t	e	n

Now check if Robin Hood's favourite sport is the first word on your list.

1. ***archery***
2. ***arrow***
3. ***bow***
4. ***competitor***
5. ***crowd***
6. ***final***
7. ***round***
8. ***shoot***
9. ***target***
10. ***winner***

4 Listening: Drama at Haywood School

4 Listen to track 4 and answer the questions.

1. What did the drama group write and act?

They wrote and acted a play about Robin Hood.

2. What did the king do in Sherwood Forest?

He hunted deer for fun.

3. What did Robin Hood do with the money from the rich people?

He gave it back to the poor people.

4. What colour did the outlaws wear in Sherwood Forest?

They wore green.

5. What part did Mr Cooper act?

Mr Cooper acted the Sheriff of Nottingham.

6. What were the Haywood outlaws carrying in the school play?

They were carrying bows and arrows.

7. What role does Mr Cooper like better than the part of the Sheriff of Nottingham?

He likes the role of German teacher better.

1 Vocabulary: Word power

1. The plural of **wife** is ___wives___ , the plural of **woman** is ___women___ .
2. **Worse** is the comparative, and **worst** is the ___superlative___ .
3. A man and a woman who love one another usually ___get married___ after some time. But some people never do. They want to stay alone.
4. When you have a really great appetite you can say: I'm ___as hungry as a horse___ .
5. The adjective is **different** and ___difference___ is the noun.
6. When you shoot an arrow you want to hit the ___bull's-eye___ .
7. When you meet a person for the first time you can say: ___Nice to meet you___ !

2 Writing: Explaining words

Put the correct parts together and link them. Use a relative pronoun or make a contact clause.

1. stage	information	show you around and ...
2. show-off	person	buy things for little money
3. table tennis	place	play on a table with a ...
4. hall	game	people act plays
5. Physial Education	room	teach sports to ...
6. bully	person	tell everybody how good ...
7. second-hand shop	place	like it if others are scared of ...
8. guide	subject	get from others about ...
9. feedback	person	meet for assembly or ...

1. A stage is a place where people act plays.
2. A show-off is a person who tells everybody how good he is.
3. Table tennis is a game you play on a table with a bat (and a ball).
4. A hall is a big room where pupils meet for assembly or for sports.
5. Physical Education is the subject which teaches sports to pupils.
6. A bully is a person who likes it if others are scared of him.
7. A second-hand shop is a place where you can buy things for little money.
8. A guide is a person who shows you around and gives you information.
9. Feedback is the information you get from others about what you did or what you said.

1 Grammar: Word order

Make positive statements (+), negative statements (–) or questions (?).
Use the correct tense: present or past, simple or progressive form.

1. (+) tea • **(have)** • usually • for breakfast • Barbara • coffee • but today • **(have)** • she
   Barbara usually has tea for breakfast, but today she's having coffee.
2. (–) David's • **(learn)** • at school • **(be)** • young • French • when • mother • she
   David's mother didn't learn French at school when she was young.
3. (?) Janet • yesterday • **(not go)** • to school • by bike • why
   Why didn't Janet go to school by bike yesterday?
4. (?) you • **(think)** • that • **(learn)** • Latin • be • difficult
   Do you think that Latin is difficult to learn?
5. (+) my father • **(try)** • his • Look • new mobile • **(use)**
   Look, my father is trying to use his new mobile.

2 Mixed bag: From David's history book

Fill in the missing words.

___In___ 1066 the Normans ___conquered___ England. Some time later, around 1190, Nottingham was a small English ___town___ of about a thousand ___people___. Sometimes they were hungry ___because___ they didn't have the right to hunt ___deer___ in the forest. When the King ___needed___ money, cruel[1] sheriffs usually ___collected___ it for him. Some Saxons couldn't ___pay___, so the sheriffs quite often ___took___ all their goods and homes. So the peasants ___became___ outlaws. The most ___famous___ of them was Robin Hood. He lived in Sherwood ___Forest___ with a group of strong men. They ___stole___ money from the ___rich___ people of Nottingham and ___gave___ it to the ___poor___ families. Two hundred years ___later___, people began to ___tell___ the first stories ___about___ Robin Hood. And today ___pupils___ still learn about ___him___ in schools.

[1] [kruəl] – grausam

Sounds good

1 Cloze test: What music do they like?

Complete the text with the following words.

all	are	band	bands'	dancing
different	doesn't	film	forty	got
great	Guitars	Her	His	is	likes
lot	music	not	Scott	She	she
their	they	three	to	when

Sarah's favourite ___band___ is Atomic Kitten. They are ___three___ girls from Liverpool who first ___got___ together in 1999. They had ___their___ first international hit in 2001. David ___likes___ rock, anything with guitars. ___Guitars___ are very important to him. ___His___ favourite band is U2. It ___doesn't___ matter to him that they ___are___ already quite old. He thinks their singer, Bono, has a ___great___ voice. 'Elevation' is the song ___they___ did for the Lara Croft ___film___ . Robert isn't very interested in ___music___ , so he never knows the ___bands'___ names. He just likes football. ___Scott___ likes to listen to hip-hop. He thinks it's great for ___dancing___, but also for saying a ___lot___ of things that you need ___to___ say. Mrs Dane's favourite music ___is___ jazz. She didn't like it ___when___ she was young, but now ___she___ thinks it's fantastic. There are ___different___ kinds of jazz and they ___all___ use different kinds of instruments, ___not___ only guitar, bass and drums. ___She___ actually likes the saxophone best. ___Her___ favourite song is already over ___forty___ years old, but she still thinks it's great.

2 Vocabulary: Funny words

Can you find the words?

1. **ieecpeerxn** ___experience___
2. **pistpoeo** ___opposite___
3. **zenese** ___sneeze___
4. **ehtlha** ___health___
5. **hcuborer** ___brochure___
6. **deaefkcb** ___feedback___
7. **ldsikie** ___dislike___
8. **htyirso** ___history___
9. **naemngi** ___meaning___
10. **eduig** ___guide___
11. **icplayhs** ___physical___
12. **ncteiudoa** ___education___

Two events

1 Grammar: *Will* or *won't*?

There is a match between Nottingham Forest and Arsenal on Friday. The Forest manager is worried. Put in *will* or *won't*.

The weather report says the weather ___will___ be bad on Friday. I hope it ___won't___ rain all day. Too much rain ___will___ ruin the grass[1] on the football field because the ground ___will___ become soft[2]. And lots of people ___won't___ come if they know they ___will___ get wet. If the fans stay at home, we ___won't___ have the money to pay our players.

I know that most of the Arsenal fans ___will___ come by train and of course, they ___will___ make a lot of noise in the city. I hope our fans ___won't___ get too excited when they see them. I'm sure we ___will___ win, but what ___will___ the fans do if we lose?

[1] [grɑːs] – Gras • [2] [sɒft] – weich

2 Grammar: The second ticket

Complete the dialogue with *will* or *won't* and mark the signal words.

tip

Signal words for the *will future*	
I expect	I'm sure
I hope	perhaps
I think	I'm afraid

Sarah: Do you think Robert ___will___ go to the concert with me? I'm afraid he ___will___ laugh at me when I ask him.
Becky: Don't be silly, Sarah. I expect he ___will___ be surprised when you ask him, but he ___won't___ laugh at you. I know he likes you.
Sarah: Perhaps he ___won't___ have time.
Becky: Maybe, but I think he ___will___ tell you, ___won't___ he?
Sarah: I expect he ___will___ watch the football match on TV. He's a big fan.
Becky: Come on, Sarah, here's my mobile. Ring him up. You ___won't___ find out what he thinks if you don't ask him.
Sarah: Oh Becky, I hope he ___won't___ make fun of me.

3 Grammar: Plans for Friday

Write down what they are going to do next Friday.

celebrate | watch | listen to | do

1. The Burtons *are going to celebrate* Grandma's birthday.
2. Robert *is going to watch a football match.*
3. Sarah and Kim *are going to listen to a concert.*
4. Mr Burton *is going to do the shopping.*

4 Grammar: A Robin Hood film

Fill in the correct tenses: present and past, simple or progressive form.

Yesterday Mum and I *watched* **(watch)** a silly Robin Hood film on TV. The best scene *was* **(be)** when the outlaws *were hiding* **(hide)** in the forest. Some of them *were lying* **(lie)** under the bushes, others *were sitting* **(sit)** in the trees when they *saw* **(see)** Maid Marian. She *was riding* **(ride)** on a horse and *was singing* **(sing)** a song, but then she *heard* **(hear)** a noise in a tree above her and a hat *fell* **(fall)** down from the tree. She *picked up* **(pick up)** the hat, *put* **(put)** it on her head at once and *shouted* **(shout)**, "Robin, I *know* **(know)** it's you! Where *are you hiding* **(you hide)**? Look, what I *bought* **(buy)** in Nottingham yesterday!" She *gave* **(give)** him a little dog. "I *think* **(think)** it will be useful in our camp," she *said* **(say)**. Then the outlaws *came* **(come)** out of the trees. We *laughed* **(laugh)** because they *looked* **(look)** so funny. They *didn't look* **(not look)** real at all. Their bows and arrows *were* **(be)** modern. Maybe they *got* **(get)** them from a toy[1] shop.

[1] [tɔɪ] – Spielzeug

1 Grammar: At the Burtons'

There is a lot of work to do before Grandma's birthday party, but everybody is friendly and will help. Use the *will future* for snap decisions.

Jobs to do
- make birthday cake ✔
- decorate living room
- not forget to give Grandma the present
- buy drinks
- invite neighbours
- go for a walk with Barker
- set table
- collect Aunt Mary at station
- not tell Grandma anything

Decide who of the Burtons wants to do what job. Start with:
All right, I'll … • Don't worry, … • Of course, … • OK, …

Mum: All right, I'll make the birthday cake.
Dad: *OK, I'll buy the drinks.*
Becky and Simon: *Don't worry, we'll decorate the living room.*
Simon: *Of course, I'll go for a walk with Barker.*
Mum: *All right, I'll invite the neighbours.*
Dad: *OK, I'll collect Aunt Mary at the station.*
Becky: *Of course, I'll set the table.*
Simon: *Don't worry, I won't tell Grandma anything.*
Becky: *Don't worry, I won't forget to give Grandma the present.*

2 Speaking: Questions

1. Peter was looking for his … . — What was Peter looking for?
2. Carina comes from … . — Where *does Carina come from*?
3. She is going to look after … . — Who *is she going to look after*?
4. The boys are interested in … . — What *are the boys interested in*?
5. He went to the cinema with … . — Who *did he go to the cinema with*?
6. Simon never plays with … . — Who *does Simon never play with*?

1 Writing: You choose

Write the correct sentences.
Put the letters of the sentences in these boxes.

A U T O G R A P H

1. Do you do (F) / Will you do (C) / Are you going to do (A) anything interesting this evening?
   Are you going to do anything interesting this evening?
2. I'm going to (U) / I'll (P) listen to a pop concert tonight.
   I'm going to listen to a pop concert tonight.
3. I hope Jim will go (T) / goes (L) / is going to go (V) with me to the concert.
   I hope Jim will go with me to the concert.
4. Are you sure the train arrives (I) / will arrive (O) / is going to arrive (D) in time?
   Are you sure the train will arrive in time?
5. How many people will we (B) / are we going to (G) / do we (D) invite to our party?
   How many people are we going to invite to our party?
6. I'm sure Harry doesn't (S) / won't (R) isn't going to (A) come anyway.
   I'm sure Harry won't come anyway.
7. Steve can't meet us now. He's working (A) / works (G) / is going to work (S).
   Steve can't meet us now. He's working.
8. Don't worry, I'm going to phone (H) / I'll phone (P) / I'm phoning (U) you soon.
   Don't worry, I'll phone you soon.
9. Do you think Jane is inviting (T) / invites (V) / will invite (H) us, too?
   Do you think Jane will invite us, too?

2 Dictation: Mr Penrose's e-mail to Mrs Croft

5 Listen to track 5 and complete the text.

Dear Sue,

This is *an invitation* for you and Robert. We *'re going to have* a garden party *at our house* in Arndale Road. It *will be* at *the end of this month*, on Saturday 24th. We *want to start* at 2.30 pm. The party is *for* Jenny Leinert *and her parents*, Helen and Martin. *As you know*, Jenny stayed with us *last year* while *her parents were still living* in Berlin. Helen Leinert is *my wife's sister*. *Now they're all here* in Nottingham. The *children are all in the same* tutor group, so it's nice to know *the families*, too. We hope the *weather* will be fine for the party and that you and Robert *will come*.

See you there, Colin Penrose

3 Mediation: In English, please

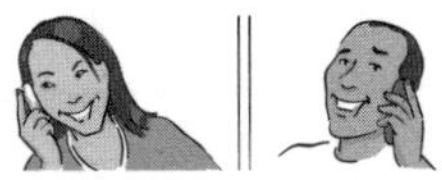

Remember that you often need future forms in English for German '*Präsens*'.

1. Kim begrüßt Lewis und teilt ihm mit, dass sie gerade am Schreibtisch sitzt und sich auf den Mathetest am Dienstag vorbereitet.
2. Lewis hofft, dass er nicht zu schwer sein wird. Er sagt, dass er letzte Woche einen Englischtest hatte und dass er OK war.
3. Sie fragt ihn, was er am Mittwochnachmittag macht. Sie möchte gern ins Kino gehen und fragt ihn, ob er auch mitkommen kann.
4. Lewis bedauert, dass er (da) nicht kann, weil er mittwochs immer Bandprobe (= *practice*) hat. Er schlägt vor, am Donnerstag ins Kino zu gehen.
5. Kim hält das für eine gute Idee und entscheidet spontan nachzuschauen, welche Filme dann laufen (= *to be on*). Sie wird ihn später wieder anrufen. Sie verabschiedet sich.

1. Hi, Lewis. I'm (just) sitting at my desk and I'm preparing for the Maths test on Tuesday.
2. I hope it won't be too difficult. I had an English test last week. It was OK.
3. What are you going to do on Wednesday afternoon? I'd like to go to the cinema. Can you come, too?
4. Sorry, I can't. I've got band practice on Wednesdays. Let's go to the cinema on Thursday.
5. That's a good idea. I'll have a look what films will be on then. I'll phone you again later. Bye.

4 Listening: Interview with a pop singer

6 Listen to track 6 and put the sentences in the right order.

1. you • Britain • like • don't • you
   You *like Britain, don't you?*
2. Nottingham • fans • my • it's • all • for • in
   It's *all for my fans in Nottingham.*
3. Saturday • concert • a • it's • special • on
   It's *a special concert on Saturday.*
4. Robin • concert • the • at • Hood • I'm • won't • be • afraid
   I'm afraid *Robin Hood won't be at the concert.*
5. six • I'm • back • morning • fly • going • on • at • to • Monday • o'clock
   I'm *going to fly back at six o'clock on Monday morning.*
6. longbow • a • take • to • I'm • back • going
   I'm *going to take a longbow back.*

unit 3 let's check

1 Speaking: Sound practice

Put the words in the right list.

also • appetite • archery • at last • at least • behind • buy • corpse • darkness • decide • detail • each • final • laugh • outlaw • piece • repeat • saw • strawberry • target

art [ɑːt]	leave [liːv]	order [ɔːdə]	hide [haɪd]
archery	at least	also	appetite
at last	detail	corpse	behind
darkness	each	outlaw	buy
laugh	piece	saw	decide
target	repeat	strawberry	final

2 Vocabulary: Puzzle time

Fill in the words.

1	PROBABLY
2	PREDICTION
3	EXERCISE
4	DRUMMER
5	DETAIL
6	DECIDE
7	DEPART
8	DESSERT
9	EXHIBITION
10	PIECE
11	PRONOUN
12	PREMIERSHIP

1. almost sure, more than perhaps
2. what you tell about the future
3. You do it for homework.
4. He plays in a band.
5. not the general information but …
6. yes or no, you must …
7. to leave
8. You eat it after the main course.
9. In an art … you see a lot of paintings.
10. A … of chocolate, please.
11. e.g. I – you – he
12. The Arsenal team wants to win it.

3 Vocabulary: Definitions

Use relative clauses or contact clauses and put in *person – dish – place – list – boy or girl.*

1. A **takeaway** is a place which / that sells meals (which / that) you can take home with you.
2. A **menu** *is a list of food (which / that) you can eat in a restaurant.*
3. A **waiter** *is a person who / that brings food and drinks in a restaurant.*
4. The **dessert** *is the dish (which / that) you eat after the main course.*
5. A **pupil** *is a boy or a girl who / that goes to school.*

Focus on food and drink

focus 2

1 Mediation: Lunch at the Burtons'

Write down what they say.

- Mrs Burton fragt Carina, ob sie etwas Suppe möchte.
- Carina stimmt zu und sagt, dass sie prima riecht.
- Mr Burton bittet höflich um das Salz.
- Becky reicht es ihm.
- Simon bittet höflich um mehr Reis.
- Mrs Burton ermuntert ihn, sich selbst zu nehmen.
- Becky fragt Carina, ob sie ihr noch mehr Fisch geben kann.
- Carina lehnt höflich ab, weil sie nicht sehr hungrig ist.
- Simon bietet spontan an, dass er den Nachtisch holt. Er fragt, wer etwas Eis möchte.

Mrs Burton: Would you like some soup, Carina?

Carina: *Yes, please. It smells super.*

Mr Burton: *Could you pass me the salt, please?*

Becky: *Here you are.*

Simon: *Could I have some more rice, please?*

Mrs Burton: *Help yourself.*

Becky: *Can I give you a little more fish, Carina?*

Carina: *No, thanks. I'm not very hungry.*

Simon: *I'll get the dessert. Who would like some ice cream?*

2 Vocabulary: A crossword puzzle

Across →

1. another word for 'very surprised' — AMAZED
4. a plan you make for the future, often with someone else — ARRANGEMENT
6. opposite of the noun 'light' — DARKNESS
11. a small book in which you write something down every day — DIARY
12. to say something again — REPEAT
13. a small word like 'in', 'after', 'at' or 'under' — PREPOSITION

Down ↓

2. This is how you feel if you hope something will happen, but it doesn't. — DISAPPOINTED
3. the first part, e.g. of a text — INTRODUCTION
5. comparative of 'bad' — WORST
7. things you throw away — RUBBISH
8. At an art … you can see lots of different pictures or paintings. — EXHIBITION
9. What will the weather be like tomorrow? – It'll … rain in the afternoon. — PROBABLY
10. the person or team that is in front of all the others — LEADER

unit 4 intro

A week in the Lake District

1 Cloze test: A week in the Lake District

Put in the missing words.

Jenny *went* to the Lake District in the *Easter* holidays with her *parents* and David. Before they left, they *packed* a lot of things and then *they* couldn't get everthing into the *car*. When Jenny was back home, she made a *scrapbook*. She put all the photos *in* it and this is what she wrote: "We stayed at a *bed* and *breakfast* place. One afternoon we *went* rowing on Derwentwater. And you often see *traffic* jams in the Lake District – not cars but sheep! You can do *lots* of adventure activities like rock *climbing*, kayaking, canoeing, *mountain* biking or pony *trekking*. We saw the Honister slate *mine*, which was fantastic. Years ago they used *ponies* and sleds to take the *slate* down the steep paths into the *valley* below. Great Gable is the 7th *highest* mountain in the Lake District. *Lots* of people go rock *climbing* there."

2 Vocabulary: Odd word out

Find the odd word out.

1	2	3	4	5
path	rowing	wine	soup	starter
valley	windsurfing	beer	pasta	dessert
steak	canoeing	jam	sled	main course
mountain	pony trekking	orange juice	rice	slate
river	kayaking	lemonade	salad	menu
rock	swimming	water	bacon	meal
steak	*pony trekking*	*jam*	*sled*	*slate*

3 Vocabulary: Definitions

Write definitions for these words.

1. traffic jam: *All the cars, buses etc. that can't move on a road.*
2. guest: *The people you invite to your house or to a party.*
3. slate: *People put slate on the roofs of their houses.*
4. to book: *You can book a room in a hotel or a bed & breakfast.*
5. to trek: *To go or walk a long way in the country.*

Ready for the holiday?

language A unit 4

1 Grammar: Before the trip

There's a lot to do before the Leinerts can leave for their holiday. First write what they are doing, and then what they have done.

1. Mr Leinert is shaving in the bathroom.
   Mr Leinert has shaved in the bathroom.
2. *Jenny is packing all her things.*
   Jenny has packed all her things.
3. *Jenny is phoning David.*
   Jenny has phoned David.
4. *Mrs Leinert is tidying the kitchen.*
   Mrs Leinert has tidied the kitchen.
5. *Mr Leinert is making sandwiches.*
   Mr Leinert has made sandwiches.
6. *The Leinerts are leaving home.*
   The Leinerts have left home.

2 Grammar: Questions and short answers

Put the verbs in the present perfect und give short answers.

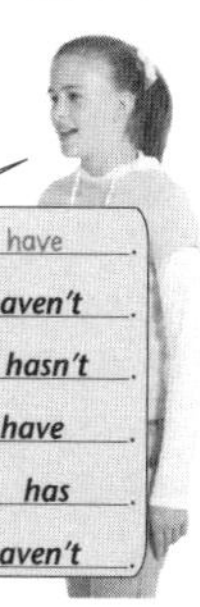

Mr Leinert:

1. Have you packed (you, pack) all your things? — Yes, I have.
2. *Have you phoned* (you, phone) David? — No, I *haven't*.
3. *Has Mum tidied* (Mum, tidy) the kitchen? — No, she *hasn't*.
4. *Have you washed* (you, wash) the dishes? — Yes, I *have*.
5. *Has Mum shut* (Mum, shut) the windows? — Yes, she *has*.
6. *Have you forgotten* (you, forget) your mobile? — No, I *haven't*.

3 Grammar: Present perfect

Write down what the Leinerts haven't done yet.

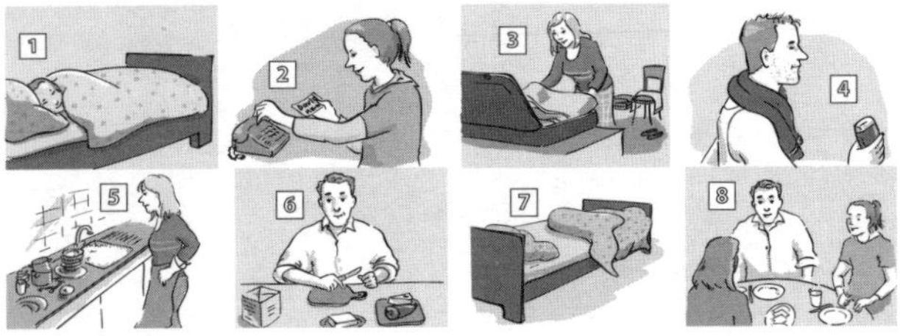

1. Jenny *hasn't got up yet.*
2. Jenny *hasn't phoned David yet.*
3. Mrs Leinert *hasn't packed her things yet.*
4. Mr Leinert *hasn't shaved yet.*
5. Mrs Leinert *hasn't washed the dishes yet.*
6. Mr Leinert *hasn't made the sandwiches yet.*
7. Jenny *hasn't made her bed yet.*
8. The Leinerts *haven't had breakfast yet.*

4 Grammar: Future forms

Put in the right future form.

1. Maybe there *will be* **(will be • is going to be)** a good film on TV this evening.
2. *Are you going to come* **(will you come • are you going to come)** to my birthday party?" – "No, I can't. But I'm sure you *will have* **(will have • are going to have)** fun."
3. "Can I play with David?" – "I'm sorry, but David *will be busy* **(will be busy • is going to be busy)** this afternoon. He *is going to clean* **(will clean • is going to clean)** his bike."
4. "What are your plans for tomorrow, David?" – "Robert and I *are going to play* **(will play • are going to play)** football together."
5. "Have you already made plans for the weekend?" – "Yes, Robert's mum *is going to get* **(will get • is going to get)** tickets for the match against Arsenal and she *is going to take* **(will take • is going to take)** us there."

1 Mediation: In English, please

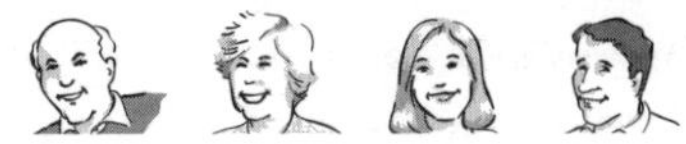

Write the dialogue.

1. Herr Preston fragt die Leinerts, ob sie jemals zuvor im Lake District gewesen sind.
2. Herr Leinert antwortet, dass er einmal vor langer Zeit als Student hier gewesen ist.
3. Frau Preston fragt Frau Leinert, ob sie schon viel herumgefahren sind und was sie bis jetzt gemacht haben.
4. Frau Leinert bejaht dies und sagt, dass sie schon das meiste des Lake Districts gesehen haben. Sie sind am Sonntag mit dem Auto herumgefahren und haben das gute Wetter ausgenutzt.
5. David sagt, dass das Wetter am Sonntag wirklich toll gewesen ist, und dass er viele Fotos gemacht hat.
6. Frau Leinert sagt, dass sie morgen den Great Gable besteigen und Ausschau nach dem Geist halten werden, besonders wenn es neblig werden wird.

Mr Preston: *Have you ever been to the Lake District before?*

Mr Leinert: *I was here once when I was a student a long time ago.*

Mrs Preston: *Have you travelled around much yet and what have you done so far?*

Mrs Leinert: *Yes, we have. We have already seen most of the Lake District. We travelled around in the car on Sunday and we made the most of the good weather.*

David: *On Sunday the weather was really great, and I took lots of photos.*

Mrs Leinert: *Tomorrow we're going to climb Great Gable and we're going to look out for the ghost, especially if it gets foggy.*

2 Grammar: Word order

Make sentences or questions. Put the verbs in the simple past or the present perfect.

1. the Lake District • **(see)** • Mr Leinert • a long time ago
   Mr Leinert saw the Lake District a long time ago.
2. **(visit)** • you • yet • the Cumberland Pencil Museum (?)
   Have you visited the Cumberland Pencil Museum yet?
3. not • David • museum • **(see)** • yet
   David hasn't seen the museum yet.
4. Mrs Preston • 1975 • **(come)** • in (?)
   Did Mrs Preston come in 1975?

5. their first day • **(travel)** around • the Leinerts • on • in the car
   On their first day the Leinerts travelled around in the car.
6. Mr Leinert • when • for the first time • **(visit)** • the Lake District (?)
   When did Mr Leinert visit the Lake District for the first time?
7. **(meet)** • just • the ghost • the Leinerts
   The Leinerts have just met the ghost.
8. never • **(be)** • before • David • to the Lakes
   David has never been to the Lakes before.
9. **(buy)** • Jenny • a box • yesterday • Cumberland pencils • of
   Jenny bought a box of Cumberland pencils yesterday.

3 Grammar: Simple past or present perfect?

David is in the Lake District. He writes a letter to his friend Mike and tells him about his holiday.
Put in the correct verb forms.

Dear Mike,

We *arrived* **(arrive)** here in the Lake District a week ago. The trip *has been* **(be)** very exciting so far. *Have* you ever *been* **(be)** to this part of Britain? Mr Leinert *stayed* **(stay)** here a long time ago when he *was* **(be)** young. I *have* never *seen* **(see)** this part of Britain. Where *did* you *spend* **(spend)** your holidays last summer?

The Leinerts are very nice. They *have shown* **(show)** me a lot of interesting things so far. I *met* **(meet)** and *spoke* **(speak)** to some nice people yesterday. Mr Preston, the owner of the bed and breakfast place, *told* **(tell)** us some exciting stories about smugglers and ghosts when we *stayed* **(stay)** with him at the weekend.

We *have just come* **(just, come)** back from a boat trip on Ullswater. Yesterday we *climbed* **(climb)** Great Gable and later in the evening we *swam* **(swim)** in the lake, which is very cold, of course. But we all *enjoyed* **(enjoy)** it.

The Leinerts *have just told* **(just, tell)** me to come in for dinner. So I must stop now. That's all for today. See you soon.

Bye, David

1 Cloze test: In the mountains

Fill in the gaps.

Yesterday Mr Preston *told* the Leinerts to be *careful* out on the mountains. He *warned* his guests because the weather *forecast* in the morning was terrible. Last year there *was* a bad *accident* up there. After the *rain* got worse and *worse*, the path became slippery. It *was* very difficult to walk. The Leinerts set *off* in the morning. Later in the afternoon it *started* to rain and it got wetter and *wetter*. After some time the Leinerts *heard* voices. They *saw* some young people *who* were wearing T-shirts. The young man's foot *was* hurt. He *needed* help immediately. Mr Leinert had his *mobile*, but he couldn't phone the *Mountain* Rescue because his battery didn't *work*. So they left their *anoraks* and followed the path down *to* the valley. Suddenly they saw the *roof* of a farm. Mr Leinert knocked at the *door* and asked the woman: "Please *call* the Mountain Rescue immediately. A man is *hurt* up in the mountains!" The Mountain Rescue people *rescued* the young people.

2 Dictation: Mrs Leinert's postcard to Mrs Penrose

7 Listen to track 7 and write the sentences.

Dear Pat,

We've arrived in the Lake District after an easy trip. There was only one traffic jam just at the end, and that was because of sheep on the road. We're staying at a lovely bed and breakfast place on Derwentwater. The sun was shining when we came, but we've all brought anoraks. We want to walk and go out in a boat on the lake, so I hope the weather will be fine. I'll see you next week,

Helen

3 Mediation: Bad weather

Say it in English. Be careful with the tenses.

1. Gestern ist die Wettervorhersage ziemlich gut gewesen, aber vielleicht wird sich das Wetter heute Nachmittag ändern.

Yesterday the weather forecast was quite good, but maybe the weather will change this afternoon.

2. Der Regen hat vor ein paar Stunden begonnen und die Wege sind sehr rutschig geworden.

The rain started a few hours ago and the paths became very slippery.

3. Wir erinnerten uns an den Unfall, von dem uns Herr Preston erzählt hat, und der letztes Jahr im März oder April geschehen ist.

We remembered the accident Mr Preston told us about which happened last year in March or April.

4 Listening: Barker's holiday in the Lake District

8 Listen to track 8 and answer these questions. When the answer is 'no', give the right information.

1. Did Barker have bacon and eggs for breakfast?

No, he didn't. He had some dog food for breakfast.

2. Did Barker go for a walk in the hotel?

No, he didn't. He jumped in the swimming pool in the hotel.

3. Were the other swimmers in the hotel happy with Barker?

No, they weren't. They were very angry with him.

4. What was Grandpa doing while Grandma was talking about Barker?

Grandpa was eating his toast.

5. Where is Barker going with Grandpa today?

He's going for a long walk to Derwentwater.

6. Is Grandpa going to paint a picture at Derwentwater?

No, he isn't. He's going to take some photographs of the boats.

7. Will Barker like swimming in Derwentwater?

Yes, he will.

1 Vocabulary: Crossword puzzle

Across →

1. the months of September, October and November
6. When you want to know what the weather will be like on the next day, you have to listen to the weather ...
7. a popular water sport you do with a boat and a paddle (not 'kayaking')
10. to move from one place to another, often as a part of a holiday
11. Obelix fell into a ... when he was young.
12. Before you go into a room you ... at the door and wait for an answer.

Down ↓

2. all the cars, buses etc. that are moving on a road
3. Something for which you have to spend a lot of money is ...
4. help that saves somebody from a dangerous situation
5. The Burtons have two children, Simon is their son and Becky is their ...
8. opposite of 'wife'
9. opposite of 'mountain'

2 Mixed bag: The ghost on Great Gable

Put in the right verb forms.

While the Leinerts *were looking for* **(suchen)** help, Jenny *saw* **(sehen)** a man in the fog. At first she *thought* **(denken)** it was her dad, so she *followed* **(folgen)** him. Suddenly the man *was* **(sein)** gone and Jenny's parents *were calling* **(rufen)** her. Later, when the Leinerts *arrived* **(ankommen)** at Moses Farm, Jenny *talked* **(sprechen)** to Mrs Moses about the man.

Jenny: "*Does your husband work* **(Ihr Mann, arbeiten)** in these mountains?"

Mrs Moses: "No, my husband *died* **(sterben)** a long time ago. Why?"

Jenny: "Oh ... sorry. Well, *have you ever met* **(Sie, schon, treffen)** a ghost here?"

Mrs Moses: "Yes, I have. Old Moses sometimes *visits* **(besuchen)** the farm. He *has lived* **(leben)** on Great Gable for hundreds of years. *Did he help* **(er, helfen)** you down the mountain?"

Jenny: "Yes, he did! He *showed* **(zeigen)** us the right path."

Mrs Moses: "You *are/were* **(sein)** lucky. Old Moses *doesn't like* **(nicht mögen)** people."

Unit 3 – Unit 4

1 Grammar: Future forms

Put in the different future forms.

1. Jenny is looking forward to her birthday. Next week she *'ll be* **(be)** twelve. David has got a plan. He *'s going to buy* **(buy)** her some nice games.
2. David is sure she *'ll like* **(like)** her presents.
3. Jenny hopes she *'ll get* **(get)** a lot of birthday presents.
4. She *'s going to invite* **(invite)** all her friends to her party. That's her plan.
5. David's parents have just decided: "We *'ll give* **(give)** Jenny a pet!"
6. David hopes they *'ll buy* **(buy)** her a dog.
7. Jenny thinks she *'ll get* **(get)** a bike for her birthday.
8. "What are your plans for the party, Jenny?" – "We *'re going to play* **(play)** football. Maybe the weather *will be* **(be)** better."

2 Mixed bag: Jenny's diary

Complete what Jenny wrote about her summer holiday in her diary.

September, 1st

This *summer* Mum and Dad *decided* to go to the *Lake District*. In the morning before *we* left there was chaos at *our* house: We *overslept* and everything went *wrong* that morning. When Mum was *tidying* the *kitchen*, Dad *dropped* the *knife* with butter on her foot. Then later, on the road, there was a terrible *traffic jam*. At the beginning the *weather* was *brilliant* and we made the most of *it* and went mountain *biking* and pony *trekking* every day. But when we decided to *climb* Great Gable, the weather *forecast* announced rain and we had to *stay* at the hotel. It was *foggy* outside, really terrible and annoying. No more rock *climbing*, no more *exciting* adventures, no more *ghosts*! We didn't *travel* around much because it got *wetter* and *wetter*. So we stayed in the *house* and watched videos. I really *hope* we will have our next *holiday* in Italy.

At Cooper Middle School

1 Vocabulary: Words and definitions

a) Find the right word.

1. If you work hard at your aims, you will probably have *success*.
2. If you don't eat enough, you'll get too *thin*.
3. Ideas and information that help you to write something are called *material*.

b) What is it in American English?

1. headmaster	*principal*	4. time table	*schedule*
2. lessons	*classes*	5. class or year	*grade*
3. programme	*program*	6. flat	*apartment*

2 Vocabulary: Cooper Middle School

Correct the wrong information.

1. Cooper Middle School is in Haywood.

Cooper Middle School is in Denver, Colorado.

2. Under 20% of Colorado adults take part in Make A Difference Day.

Under 20% of Colorado adults are overweight.

3. The 'Mile High City' is at the foot of Dinosaur Ridge.

The 'Mile High City' is at the foot of the Rocky Mountains.

4. Denver is the 'green city' because most of the public buildings are green.

Denver is the 'green city' because it has the largest city park system in the US.

3 Vocabulary: School activities

Explain what you do in these clubs.

a) Semantics: *In Semantics you learn where words come from and how to spell them.*

b) Earth Keepers Club: *In the Earth Keepers Club you can do something for our world.*

c) Drama Club: *In the Drama Club you can act plays in English or Spanish.*

1 Mixed bag: Making plans

Complete the dialogue between Ms Gerlernter and her students with the words and phrases from one of the three boxes. The numbers show you in which box you'll find the answer.

1 German	2 Verbs	3 Phrases
Gemeinde	give	anyway
herumhängen	like	come on
langweilig	look	don't worry
Leute ✔	give	great idea
Müll	not do	how about
nicht wahr?	need	I guess
pflanzen	give	I'm sure
vor	sound	no, thanks
wenigstens	have	wait a minute
Säcke	do	don't know

Ms G: What are you ___guys___ (1) going to do on Make A Difference Day?

José: Maybe we could ___plant___ (1) some trees ___in front of___ (1) the school building. If we do that, then the front ___will___ ___look___ (2) much more interesting.

Ms G: ___Great idea___ (3). It really looks ___boring___ (1) out there. But ___I guess___ (3) you ___will need___ (2) some money for that, ___won't you___ (1)? ___How about___ (3) asking your parents for some? If they ___give___ (2) you some money, I ___'ll give___ (2) you the tools.

Bruce: Hmm! I ___don't know___ (3). ___Anyway___ (3), why don't we just go to Washington Park then and pick up ___trash___ (1)?

Tina: Oh, ___wait a minute___ (3), I ___'m not going to do___ (2) that. That really ___sounds___ (2) like hard work. ___No, thanks___ (3)! Forget it.

José: ___Come on___ (3), Tina. Do you just want to ___hang around___ (1)?

Ms G: Well, ___I'm sure___ (3) your parents ___will like___ (2) it if you ___do___ (2) something like that for the ___community___ (1), Tina.

Tina: And what about the ___bags___ (1)? We will need ___at least___ (1) ten.

Ms G.: ___Don't worry___ (3) about that. Mr Weinberger ___will give___ (2) you all you need.

Bruce: OK. I think we ___have___ (2) a plan now.

2 Grammar: New in Denver

Use the correct verb form and complete the sentences.

Donna: If I ___go___ **(go)** to CMS next year, I ___'ll join___ **(join)** their girls' soccer team.

Dad: That's a good idea. If you ___do___ **(do)** that, you ___'ll be___ **(be)** a superstar in a month.

Donna: Come on, Dad. Don't be silly. But I'm sure that the team ___will have___ **(have)** a lot of success if we all ___work___ **(work)** together.

Dad: And if you ___aren't___ **(not be)** successful, ___will you join___ **(you, join)** the Players then?

Donna: The Players? You mean the drama group?

Dad: Yes, they're great. If they ___find___ **(find)** out how good you are, they ___'ll give___ **(give)** you a big part in their next school play. And if there ___is___ **(be)** someone from Hollywood – and sometimes there is – they ___'ll offer___ **(offer)** you a role in a film, and if the film ___becomes___ **(become)** a success, you ___'ll be___ **(be)** a …

Donna: Dad, if you ___say___ **(say)** that word again, I ___'ll leave___ **(leave)** Denver and never ___come___ **(come)** back!

3 Writing: Make sentences

Match the parts of the sentences and write them down.

If José and the others pick up trash	I won't answer the phone.
If they ask their parents for help	she won't play in the next game.
When I do my assignment tomorrow morning	they'll need a lot of bags.
When school starts in fall	they'll give them some money.
If Joanne is late for practice	she'll buy some candy.
When Sally goes to the supermarket tomorrow	Donna will be a student at CMS.

1. If José and the others pick up trash, they'll need a lot of bags.
2. *If they ask their parents for help, they'll give them some money.*
3. *When I do my assignment tomorrow morning, I won't answer the phone.*
4. *When school starts in fall, Donna will be a student at CMS.*
5. *If Joanne is late for practice, she won't play in the next game.*
6. *When Sally goes to the supermarket tomorrow, she'll buy some candy.*

1 Grammar: When you are grown up …

What will you ***be allowed to do***, what will you ***have to do*** and what won't you ***have to do*** when you are grown up?

drive a car

go to school

buy your own clothes

work long hours

do homework

go to wild parties

1. When I'm grown up, I'll be allowed to drive a car.
2. *When I'm grown up, I won't have to go to school.*
3. *When I'm grown up, I'll be allowed to buy my own clothes.*
4. *When I'm grown up, I'll have to work long hours.*
5. *When I'm grown up, I won't have to do homework.*
6. *When I'm grown up, I'll be allowed to go to wild parties.*

2 Grammar: Substitute forms

Change the following sentences into a) the past tense and b) the future.

1. The 7th graders can organize a bazaar, but they must ask Ms Gerlernter first.

a) The 7th graders were allowed to organize a bazaar, but they had to ask Ms Gerlernter first.

b) *The 7th graders will be allowed to organize a bazaar, but they'll have to ask Ms Gerlernter first.*

2. Sally and her friends can collect some money for the hospital.

a) *Sally and her friends were able to collect some money for the hospital.*

b) *Sally and her friends will be able to collect some money for the hospital.*

3. Donna needn't do her homework because of her project.

a) *Donna didn't have to do her homework because of her project.*

b) *Donna won't have to do her homework because of her project.*

4. Sven and Bruce mustn't miss more than two classes on Monday morning.

a) *Sven and Bruce weren't allowed to miss more than two classes on Monday morning.*

b) *Sven and Bruce won't be allowed to miss more than two classes on Monday morning.*

3 Mediation: An e-mail to Sven

Write an e-mail to Sven and get some information about his latest 'Make A Difference Day' project.

1. Begrüße Sven und teile ihm mit, warum du schreibst.
2. Berichte, dass deine Klasse die Erlaubnis hat, ein Projekt mit einem Wohltätigkeitsverein deiner Stadt zu machen.
3. Frage ihn, welches Projekt er und seine Klasse dieses Jahr in Denver gemacht haben, ob die Schüler in seiner Klasse in der Lage gewesen sind, sich auf ein Projekt zu einigen, was sie machen mussten, um genügend Geld zu sammeln und ob er und seine Freunde damit armen Familien in ihrer Gemeinde helfen konnten.

Hi Sven,

How are you doing? I'm writing to ask you about your latest 'Make A Difference Day' project. My class is allowed to do a project with some people from a charity here in … What kind of project did you do in Denver this year? Were the students in your class able to agree on one project? And what did you guys have to do to collect enough money? Were you and your friends able to help poor families in your community with it?

Bye for now, …

1 Vocabulary: Word families

Find a verb or an adjective from the same word family.

1. introduction	*to introduce*	6. noise	*noisy*
2. difference	*different*	7. fog	*foggy*
3. truth	*true*	8. day	*daily*
4. invitation	*to invite*	9. winner	*to win*
5. definitions	*definite*	10. shot	*to shoot*

2 Cloze test: Joanne's story

Fill in the gaps.

Now everybody is angry with *me*. They all think I'm a *crazy* jerk or something like that. *And* all this because I played *a* little joke on Tina and *José*. Tina really asked for it *because* she always thinks that she *is* Miss Wonderful. You know, I *really* wanted that part in the *school* play. I thought: If I *get* this role, I will be *the* star of the show. But *then* Tina smiled at Mr Carpeletti *and* that was it. So she *got* the part, and what is *worse*, her acting was really brilliant. *Anyway*, José is crazy about Tina, *too*, like the rest of the *world*. He has only got eyes *for* her. I'm not jealous *of* her, believe me. Maybe I *should* talk to José about the *mess* and explain to him why *I* did what I did. I'm *sure* he'll understand.

3 Writing: Donna's diary

In her diary, Donna presents a number of different characters. Bruce Csonka is one of them. Does he have a reason to hurt Tina and José? And does he have the chance to do so? Write about 60–70 words to answer these questions.

Before José's review of the play, Bruce was crazy about Tina and she always hung around with him. But the guy Tina really likes is José, and I think Bruce knows it. So I think he had a reason to hurt Tina and José. And, of course, it was Bruce who did the layout. So he had enough time to change José's review before it went off to the printer.

4 Dictation: Acrobats

9 Listen to track 9 and complete the text.

Have you *ever seen* acrobats *on stage* or on TV? What they do is *very exciting* and takes many *years of practice*. They *juggle* with balls or other things *which they throw* to each other very *fast*. Some acrobats throw things *that are dangerous*, like *knives*, or things *that can break*, like *plates*. They can *dance and juggle* at the same time, or use their feet to throw and turn things *in the air*. *Although* their tricks are difficult, *they smile* all the time. *While you're watching* you think "*I'd like to do that*," but then you see *how difficult it is* and *how much work* they do.

5 Listening: Make a Difference Day

10 Listen to track 10 and answer the questions.

1. Who was busy while the students were working on their projects?
   Some of the teachers.
2. Who designed special pages for the website?
   Mr Weinberger.
3. What did Ms Kellermann organize?
   Ms Kellermann organized a party for all the students.
4. Who took photos of all the students?
   Mr Weinberger took photos of all the students.
5. Why was the teachers' play a play with a difference?
   It was a play with a difference because nearly everything went wrong.
6. Which instrument did Mr Weinberger play in the teachers' band?
   He played the trumpet.
7. Which stories did Ms Kellermann say she preferred?
   Ms Kellermann preferred stories about Robin Hood and the Sheriff of Nottingham.
8. Why does José want another Make a Difference Day party?
   He wants to see if Mr Weinberger has practiced the trumpet since the last party.

1 Mixed bag: José, the mariachi player

Fill in the gaps.

José Fernandez *plays* the trumpet in his dad's mariachi *band*. He has played the trumpet since *he* was five years old and he has *become* a fantastic mariachi artist by *now*. One can really say he has *made* the most of it because in *the* beginning he had to practice a *lot* and sometimes he was quite unhappy *about* it. Actually, it made him angry *when* he had to hang around in the house *and* play the same old songs over and over again *while* his friends were allowed to *play* soccer or do something else outside. Sometimes *he* was so bored that he wanted to *throw* his trumpet against the wall. But because his *father* taught him a feeling of obligation, *he* finally got past the elementary difficulties *and* began to enjoy playing his instrument. Now he *can't* imagine a life without his trumpet.

2 Mediation: School rules

Your American penfriend has sent you an e-mail in which he asks you to give him some information about the rules at your school. Write an answer and use these notes.

- Schüler müssen pünktlich zum Unterricht in den Klassenzimmern sein.
- Es ist den Schülern nicht erlaubt, in den Klassenzimmern zu essen. Einige Lehrer erlauben ihnen aber, etwas zu trinken.
- Die Schüler müssen den ganzen Vormittag in der Schule bleiben.
- Und auf dem Schulgelände dürfen sie nicht rauchen (= *to smoke*).

Hi Chris,

Thank you for your e-mail. You wanted to know *something about rules at my school. So here you go! At my school students have to be in their classrooms before classes start. They aren't allowed to eat in the classrooms. Some teachers, however, allow them to drink something. Students have to stay at school the whole morning. And they aren't allowed to smoke on the school grounds. That's it.*

Bye for now, …

Focus on travel and transport

1 Vocabulary: Definitions

1. check-in: *The place at the airport where you show your ticket and leave your big bags.*
2. boarding pass: *It looks like a ticket and shows that you're allowed to get on the plane.*
3. departure: *The time when a flight or a train leaves.*

2 Writing: Means of transport

You are in New York City and want to travel to San Francisco on the west coast. Name three possible means of transport and describe the positive and negative points of each. Use if-clauses.

a) I can go by train. If I go by train, *it'll take almost three days to get there. But it'll be much cheaper than to go by plane (and I will see a lot of the country).*

b) *I can also go by bus. If I go by bus, I'll meet lots of other passengers. I'll be able to talk to them and have fun. (But if I sit next to an unfriendly person, the ride will be quite boring.)*

c) *And I can go by car. If I do that, I can stop where and when I like to. But If I use the car, I won't meet any interesting people (and I'll need a lot of gas).*

3 Mediation: At SeaTac Airport

You are going to spend a few weeks with your aunt and uncle in Los Angeles. You're at SeaTac Airport in Seattle at the moment and are talking to Aunt Sue on the phone.

1. Teile deiner Tante mit, wo du gerade bist und dass du mit dem Flugzeug nach LA kommen wirst. Die Flugdauer wird etwa drei Stunden betragen und du wirst um 18 Uhr in LA sein.
   Hi, Aunt Sue. I'm at SeaTac Airport in Seattle at the moment. I'm going to take the plane to LA The flight takes about three hours. I'll be in LA by six o'clock.
2. Als deine Tante dich fragt, warum du deine Pläne geändert hast, sagst du, dass du ursprünglich die Strecke von Seattle nach LA mit dem Bus zurücklegen wolltest, dass aber schwere Regenfälle in den Rocky Mountains zu Schwierigkeiten für Busreisende geführt haben.
   I wanted to take the bus from Seattle to LA, but heavy rain in the Rocky Mountains has made it difficult to travel by bus.
3. Du fügst hinzu, dass die Busse von Seattle nach LA mehrere Stunden Verspätung haben und du deshalb denkst, dass das Flugzeug doch der einfachste Weg für die weite Strecke sein wird.
   The buses from Seattle to LA are delayed several hours. So I think the plane will be the easiest way for the long distance.

In the country

1 Mixed bag: The brochure

Put in the missing words.

Visit the Lazy G!

There are many *reasons* to come here: The Lazy G is not only a *guest* ranch, it is a real *cattle* ranch, too. You will be *allowed* to take part *in* every aspect of ranch life. Branding and *roping* are only two of them. We have got over 600 cows and *calves* on 15,000 acres of land right in the heart of the Rocky *Mountains*. We can *offer* you a lot of exciting *activities*, for example *horseback* riding, camping *trips* or *trout* fishing in one of our clean rivers. If you want to go riding, you need to bring some *gear*: a hat, one or two pairs of jeans, a *light* jacket and cowboy *boots*. (*Break* them in first!) You don't need your own *saddle* or chaps and remember that you mustn't use *spurs*. Our horses move without them! We are *located* near Billings where there is an *airport*. Why don't you *join* us for a week of western fun?

2 Cloze test: A letter

Karen Thompson is a guest at the Lazy G. She writes a letter to her husband. Fill in the gaps.

Dear Steve,

I hope you're fine and you don't *have* to work too hard. I'm enjoying my ranch *vacation* very much. Ed and Martha Gooch are lovely *people*, the food is simple but delicious and the *horses* are very easy to ride. From my room I *have* got a beautiful view of the Rocky Mountains. Last *night* we had a square dance evening. I danced all night, *but* you needn't be jealous – my partner was an old cowboy. *He* is seventy-two, but he can dance a lot better *than* most younger men. I really like country music. Today I *joined* the cowboys on a cattle drive. It was really *exciting*. My horse Rusty was the best horse I have ever *ridden*. I have just noticed that in another week I'll *have* to work at the bank again. I hate the idea. *Next* year you will have to try and come, too. Laura would *like* it here, too. Say hello to my little girl *for* me. Love to both of you,

Karen

At the Lazy G

1 Grammar: Indefinite pronouns

Ed, Martha, Sally Gooch and Chuck Miller are having dinner at the Lazy G. Put in *some* or *any*.

Martha: You must be hungry. We've got tomato soup tonight. Here's *some* bread to go with it. Then we have steak and chips …

Ed: Aren't there *any* potatoes?

Martha: Of course, there are *some* potatoes for you. I know you don't like chips. Can I go on now?

Ed: Of course, you can. Sorry.

Martha: Well, here's *some* salad because we haven't got *any* vegetables today …

Sally: Haven't we got *any* dessert?

Martha: You're as bad as your uncle, Sally. No, we haven't got *any*.

Sally/Ed: Oh, no!

Chuck: Don't worry. She's joking. I saw a huge bowl of strawberries in the kitchen.

Sally/Ed: Ah!

Martha: Chuck is right. We're going to have strawberries and cream for dessert. Would you like *some*?

Sally/Ed: Of course!

Martha: Okay, but you must wait a little bit. Now, who would like to start with *some* soup? You, Sally?

Sally: Yes, thank you. But I don't want *any* bread. I need room for the strawberries.

2 Grammar: What is the right compound?

Put in: every- some- any- no-

1. I can't find my cap. I know I had it when I came home. So it must be *some*where.
2. I can't find my cap. Where can it be? I've looked for it *every*where.
3. I can't find my cap *any*where.
4. Chuck really likes his state, Texas. I think he knows *every*thing about it.
5. Mr Holden thinks people in Montana speak like Chuck. He knows *no*thing about Montana.

3 Grammar: An accident on a cattle drive

Put in *some, any, every, no* or their compounds.

some any every no

Mr Holden: Stop, you stupid horse. Whoa! Help!

Chuck: Don't fall off! Hold on! Oops – too late. Are you OK, Mr Holden?

Mr Holden: No, I'm not OK. I can't see *anything* because there's sand in my eyes. I feel pain[1] *everywhere*. I think I broke my legs and arms. Isn't *anybody* going to help me?

Chuck: Well, I don't think your arms are broken – the way you're waving them about. Let me have a look at your legs. Can you move them? That's good. There's *nothing* wrong with you.

Mr Holden: That's what you think. I think I must go to the hospital at once.

Chuck: Let's find out if you can get up first. Can *somebody* come and give me a hand? Thanks, Sally. Let's help Mr Holden to get up.

Mr Holden: Oh, that rude[2] girl. I don't want her *anywhere* near me!

Chuck: Sally is a nice young lady, Mr Holden. She'll help you. That's it, Mr Holden. See? You can stand. *Everything* is going to be OK.

Mr Holden: Well, maybe I can stand, but I'm not going to ride that horse any more. He's dangerous.

Sally: He's not! You can't find a better horse *anywhere*, but you have to treat him right.

Chuck: Easy, Miss Sally. Sorry, Mr Holden, if you don't want to ride Rusty again, choose one of the other horses. You can take *any* horse you like.

Mr Holden: Then I'll take your horse. But I can tell you one thing. I'm going to spend my next summer vacation *somewhere* in Florida. No more ranch vacations for me!

[1] [peɪn] – Schmerz • [2] [ruːd] – unverschämt

Mr Holden writes a letter

1 Writing: Make sentences

Match the parts of the sentences and write them down.

Suddenly I realized	trying although it is difficult.
He spoke with	your horse right, you won't have problems.
Keep	forward to our week at the ranch.
When you treat	to the waiter because my omelette didn't come.
We're all looking	that I needed a break.
I had to complain	to be late. He's never on time.
I expected him	a strong accent.

Suddenly I realized that I needed a break.

He spoke with a strong accent.

Keep trying although it is difficult.

When you treat your horse right, you won't have problems.

We're all looking forward to our week at the ranch.

I had to complain to the waiter because my omelette didn't come.

I expected him to be late. He's never on time.

2 Grammar: Mr Holden's accident

Put in the correct verb forms and be careful with the tenses.

1. If Mr Holden *goes* **(go)** to Florida next year, he *will be able to lie* **(can, lie)** on the beach all day.
2. Last night Chuck *had to tell* **(must, tell)** Ed Gooch about Mr Holden's accident.
3. Sally *didn't have to worry* **(needn't, worry)** about Rusty because everybody knew that Rusty was a good horse.
4. If a rider *treats* **(treat)** Rusty right, he *will have* **(have)** a wonderful horse.
5. When Mr Holden came home, he told his friends: "Can you imagine? I *wasn't allowed* **(can't, use)** spurs on that ranch. You can't tell a horse who's boss *to use* without them."
6. Chuck rode Rusty the day after Mr Holden's accident and he *didn't have to use* **(needn't, use)** spurs to tell Rusty what to do.

3 Writing: You want to complain

You're spending your summer vacation in a terrible hotel, although their brochure promised you a wonderful vacation. Complain to the owner of the hotel – he isn't very friendly. Write the dialogue.

That's what the brochure says	That's why you complain
• hotel not far from the beach	• fish and chips every day, no salad
• big swimming pool	• room with a view of the road
• room with a view of the sea	• noisy parties every night
• good food	• must walk 15 minutes to beach
• quiet hotel	• swimming pool very small and not clean

You: I'm not enjoying my summer vacation! *Your brochure says that your hotel isn't far from the beach, but I must walk 15 minutes to get there. And my room doesn't have a view of the sea. When I look out of my window, I can only see the road.*

Owner: Well, 15 minutes isn't far, an hour is far. And the road is the road to the beach. Why are you complaining?

You: *There are other things, too. You say this hotel is a quiet hotel, but there are noisy parties every night and I can't sleep.*

Owner: My other guests are enjoying their vacation. That's why they always have parties. Why don't you go to the parties, too?

You: *What about your good food? It's fish and chips every day. There is never a salad.*

Owner: The fish is good, and the chips are good. A lot of people don't like salad.

You: *And what about your big swimming pool? It's very small and it isn't very clean.*

Owner: It's big enough for the children and I think it's clean.

1 Writing: For and against

Is a vacation in Florida really better than a ranch vacation in Montana? Here are some arguments. Make notes and put them in the right list. Then write a letter to Mr Holden and tell him what you think.

1. You can relax and lie on the beach in Florida.
2. The weather in Florida is usually better than in Montana, especially in the fall.
3. There are not so many tourists in Montana, so there are no crowds.
4. You learn how people live on a ranch.
5. Summers in Florida can be very hot, so hot that you won't want to leave your hotel room.
6. Some of the activities at a ranch can be dangerous when you come from a city.
7. There are lots of fun activities like swimming, windsurfing, fishing or you can go on a boat trip.
8. The Rocky Mountains are very beautiful.

A vacation in Florida is better than a ranch vacation in Montana.

For	Against
• relax and lie on the beach	• not so many tourists in Montana
• *weather usually better, especially in fall*	• *learn how people live on a ranch*
• *ranch activities dangerous*	• *Florida is too hot in summer, can't leave hotel room*
• *swimming, windsurfing, fishing or boat trip*	• *Rocky Mountains are beautiful*

Dear Mr Holden,

I have heard that you don't want to spend your vacation on a guest ranch any more. Is it true that you want to go to Florida next summer? In my opinion *a ranch vacation is much more interesting than a vacation in Florida. You can do lots of things like horseback riding or fishing. When you help with roping and branding, you find out how people in Montana really live. The weather is better for you, too. Of course, there is sometimes a little rain, but it's usually not as hot as in Florida. The Rocky Mountains are fantastic. The plains and canyons are very beautiful and there are not as many tourists as in Florida. //*

In my opinion *that's a very good idea. The weather in Florida is usually much nicer than in Montana and there are lots of things to do. You can be lazy and just lie on the beach, but if you want to take part in some activities, you can do that, too. There is swimming and windsurfing. You can also go on a boat trip if you like. All this is fun and it's a lot safer than horseback riding or taking part in cattle drives. I would go to Florida, too.*

Yours,

2 Dictation: The guest book

11 Listen to track 11 and write down what Mr Holden wrote in the guest book at the Lazy G.

I only stayed here for one week, but it felt like a much longer time. I can ride, I've had lessons. But the horse I had here was too small for me and too slow. I couldn't make it move. I wanted to wear spurs but I was not allowed to. I didn't like my room. The bed was hard and the door squeaked. How can you relax on vacation when there's so much to complain about?

3 Mixed bag: Rodeos

Fill in the gaps.

Many people enjoy going to *rodeos*. They think they can see real *cowboys* there and don't realize that they're *only* shows. Of course, it's fun to watch the *barrel* races. Horse and rider must go as *fast* as they can round three colored *barrels*. When a horse knocks a barrel *over*, there is a time penalty. The *crowds* cheer for the best horses and riders. But actually, a *lot* of those horses get hurt. You never hear *what* happens to them later.

4 Listening: Welcome to Yellowstone Park

12 Listen to track 12 and finish these statements.

1. You'd love it here. We do great trips *on* *horseback*.
2. If there's somewhere special you would like to see, we can do a special *day* *trip* *just* *for* *you*.
3. We can also take you for wonderful walks to look for *wild* *animals* *and* *birds*.
4. Are you going to take a winter *vacation* *this* *year*?
5. We also have restaurants where the *food* *is* *very* *good*.
6. There's such a lot to do in Yellowstone Park every *month* *of* *the* *year*.
7. Come and enjoy *the* *Yellowstone* *experience*.

1 Vocabulary: Crossword Puzzle

Find the words and put them in.

Across →

2. It's another word for 'mad'.
4. When you don't like people because they are better than you, then you are …
6. You haven't got much room on the left or the right in a … canyon.
8. This is a word for all the animals that don't live in zoos, people's homes or on farms.
9. If you … somebody, you believe that the person is good and won't hurt you.
11. You use them to explain the reasons for your opinion.
14. Is this ring made of … gold or does it only look like it?
15. The … is ringing. The lesson is over now.

Down ↓

1. You are … when you do things others are too frightened to do.
3. It is a word made of two other words, for example some + thing.
5. You wear it over your pullover or sweatshirt. It's shorter than a coat.
7. To say that your opinion is different.
10. This is not a good road. It is so … that I move up and down in my seat when I use it.
12. When you … what a situation is like, you understand why it is like that.
13. I know the words of this song but not the …, so I can't sing it.

2 Vocabulary: Odd word out

Decide which word is the odd word out and explain in one sentence why you think so.

1	2	3	4	5
budgie	spurs	plain	saucer	nervous
dog	saddle	kitchen	salad	frightened
bear	chaps	mountain	sandwich	excited
cat	laptop	valley	sausage	terrified

1. Bear is the odd word out because a bear is a wild animal (the other animals are pets).
2. *Laptop is the odd word out because you don't need a laptop to go horseback riding.*
3. *Kitchen is the odd word out because it's in a house.*
4. *Saucer is the odd word out because you can't eat a saucer.*
5. *Excited is the odd word out because it's nice to be excited.*

Unit 5 – Unit 6

1 Vocabulary: Prepositions

in | of | into | to | over | on

Put in the missing prepositions. You must use some of them more than once.

1. This steak is huge. Divide it ___*into*___ two pieces. You can have one of them.
2. You aren't wearing your glasses. Be careful. Don't knock ___*over*___ that mug.
3. I'll leave your book with our neighbours ___*in*___ case we're out when you come.
4. "What's that noise?" – "Oh, my sister is screaming. She has seen a spider and she is frightened ___*of*___ spiders."
5. Are you looking forward ___*to*___ your ranch vacation?
6. Why are you complaining ___*to*___ me? I didn't tell you to do these exercises.
7. If you don't want to wear these old T-shirts again, get rid ___*of*___ them.
8. Tie your dog ___*to*___ that post over there. You can't take it into the shop.
9. Is the flight ___*on*___ time or is it delayed?
10. Why don't you take part ___*in*___ the project at school?

2 Cloze test: A problem with a calf

Fill in the gaps.

The cows in Montana have a very ___*happy*___ life. They're not in a shed, ___*but*___ outside on the plains in the beautiful ___*Rocky*___ Mountains. Their calves can drink their mothers' ___*milk*___ and can play with other calves. But ___*life*___ in the mountains can be dangerous, too. ___*Sometimes*___ bears or cougars try to kill a calf. ___*They*___ usually can't do it, but they frighten the ___*cattle*___ and then they run away. That is what ___*happened*___ on the day Sally arrived. Chuck rang Martha to ___*tell*___ her that a calf was lying in a narrow canyon. ___*Its*___ leg was broken. Martha and Ed immediately ___*drove*___ to the canyon in their pickup. Ed climbed down to the ___*calf*___ and tied a rope round it. He and Chuck ___*pulled*___ the little animal up. They put it on the ___*pickup*___ and drove home. Sally phoned the vet. He ___*looked*___ after the calf. Chuck brought the calf's ___*mother*___ to the ranch. Now they are living in a corral ___*until*___ the calf is OK again.

Heroes and heroines

1 Writing: Who is it?

Explain the link between the two words. Which of the characters on page 84/85 in your textbook is described here? Use the character's name in your sentence.

1. bird • ball

A bird helps Cinderella to go to a ball where a prince falls in love with her.

2. Mississippi • adventures

Tom Sawyer and Huckleberry Finn live in a Mississippi River town and experience adventures together in the 1840s.

3. fight • crime

Batman and his friend Robin fight the terrible crime in Gotham City.

4. athletic • archaeology

Lara Croft is very athletic and loves archaeology.

5. Native American chief • English colonist

Pocahontas was the daughter of a Native American chief and married an English colonist.

6. magic • Lord Voldemort

Harry Potter uses magic to save the world from Lord Voldemort.

2 Vocabulary: Word puzzle

Find nine (+ two) words that have to do with the heroes and heroines.

1. *wizard*
2. *modern*
3. *crime*
4. *evil*
5. *stepsisters*
6. *athletic*
7. *colonist*
8. *identity*
9. *archaeology (cruel, chief)*

C	P	W	I	Z	A	R	D	I	E	R	W
A	R	H	S	A	O	F	S	D	X	Z	A
R	I	U	T	T	I	O	C	E	J	N	R
T	N	W	E	H	U	L	O	N	E	W	C
M	C	G	P	L	M	N	L	T	V	C	H
B	E	B	S	E	C	S	O	I	Q	L	A
P	P	J	I	T	M	H	N	T	K	V	E
Q	L	S	S	I	E	A	I	Y	C	B	O
Y	K	A	T	C	L	I	S	E	R	W	L
M	O	D	E	R	N	V	T	B	F	C	O
X	D	C	R	I	M	E	V	I	L	A	G
C	E	R	S	E	A	C	N	M	P	I	Y

A party

1 Grammar: Adjectives and adverbs

Do you remember this dialogue in your textbook? Fill in the missing adjectives and adverbs. Then underline the adjectives in blue and the adverbs in red.

Bruce: Come in, Donna! Wow, look at you! You're Lara Croft, right?

Donna: Yes, I am. Who are you?

Bruce: Oh come on, that's an ___*easy*___ question to answer. Everyone else recognized me ___*easily*___ enough. Isn't it ___*clear*___ from the clues? British school uniform. Scar over my eyes.

Donna: Oh, that's a scar. I couldn't see it ___*clearly*___ at first. You're Harry Potter!

Bruce: ___*Clever*___ girl! And my friend Hermione is somewhere at the party, too.

Donna: Oh yes, there she is. It's Tina. Hey, and there's Otis as Superman. And who's that as Batman?

Bruce: It's José. He's made his costume very ___*cleverly*___, hasn't he? But let's go and say hello to Sally – I mean, the Joker. She's standing all alone.

Donna: Hi, Joker. I can see why nobody is talking to you. You're smiling so ___*nastily*___!

Sally: Because I *am* ___*nasty*___. I'm a ___*bad*___ guy!

Bruce: Well, please don't behave ___*badly*___ at my party.

Sally: OK. It'll be a ___*hard*___ job, but I'll try ___*hard*___ to be ___*nice*___ to everybody.

Bruce: Here's your chance now, Joker. Look, Batman is coming over here.

Sally: Hi, Batman. How are you this evening? What ___*beautiful*___ ears you have! Would you like to dance with me? I'm sure you dance ___*beautifully*___.

José: Huh? What's going on here? Is this the Joker I love to hate?

Donna: He's trying to be ___*friendly*___. Say yes, Batman! Say it ___*fast*___, before he changes his mind!

José: Er – OK. Why not? But don't play any tricks on me while we're dancing, Joker.

Donna: Ha, ha! This is a ___*good*___ party, Bruce. You've organized it really ___*well*___.

Bruce: Come on. Let's dance, too. This is ___*nice*___ ___*fast*___ music – just the thing for ___*athletic*___ Lara Croft!

2 Grammar: Adjectives and adverbs

Read what Sally says. While you're reading, underline the adjectives in blue and the adverbs in red. Write them in the right list.

"Donna and I were invited to Bruce's party. I was dressed as Batman and my costume was really cool. Donna was a fantastic Cinderella. Her long dress was really beautiful and everybody recognized her easily. While we were dancing crazily, Donna suddenly screamed loudly. 'There's something under my dress! It's attacking me wildly!' I turned around too quickly to see why Donna was screaming and I fell to the floor with a loud bang. Luckily, I wasn't hurt badly. Everybody else came to Donna and me excitedly to see what was going on. While I was lying on the floor, I saw the dangerous monster, which was attacking the pretty Cinderella – it was Bruce's cat Susie! The poor thing was so frightened that she ran off fast. Soon we were all laughing merrily because it was such a funny situation. 'You aren't a very realistic Cinderella,' I said to Donna, 'Cinderella isn't afraid of animals, she loves them!'"

Adjectives	Adverbs
cool, *fantastic, long, beautiful, loud,*	easily, *crazily, loudly, wildly, quickly,*
dangerous, pretty, poor, frightened, funny,	*badly, excitedly, fast, merrily*
realistic, afraid	

3 Writing: If I could do magic

What would these characters say if they could do magic? Find the correct word order and make adverbs from the adjectives.

1. *Harry Potter to Lord Voldemort:*

not • world • treat • **(bad)** • the ••• otherwise • fight • I • you • will • **(brave)**

Don't treat the world badly. Otherwise I will fight you bravely.

2. *Cinderella to her stepsisters:*

me • laugh • **(nasty)** • not • at ••• otherwise • you • have to • clean • my shoes • will • **(careful)**

Don't laugh nastily at me. Otherwise you will have to clean my shoes carefully.

3. *Tom Sawyer to his Aunt Polly:*

not • at • shout • **(angry)** • me ••• otherwise • I • run • **(far)** • will • away

Don't shout at me angrily. Otherwise I will run far away.

4. *Batman to the Joker:*

smile • not • **(broadly)** ••• have to • you • otherwise • escape • will • **(fast)**

Don't smile broadly. Otherwise you will have to escape fast.

5. *Pocahontas to the English colonists:*

people • my • against • fight • not • **(hard)** ••• attack • we • otherwise • you • **(regular)** • will

Don't fight hard against my people. Otherwise we will attack you regularly.

6. *Lara Croft to an enemy:*

not • scream • **(loud)** ••• I • into • you • change • can • a • **(easy)** • frog

Don't scream loudly. I can change you into a frog easily.

4 Grammar: A party

What are these people doing at the party? Use an adverb to describe how they are doing it. The adjectives on the right can help you. What do you think the situation is?

quick · broad · loud · careful · crazy · fast

1. A girl is preparing a salad quickly. Maybe she's a bit late.
2. *A boy is dancing/jumping around crazily. Maybe he's listening to his favourite song.*
3. *A boy is smiling broadly. Maybe he has fallen in love.*
4. *A girl is carrying drinks carefully. Maybe she has already dropped some of them.*
5. *A girl is singing loudly. Maybe she loves the song.*
6. *A boy is eating his cake fast. Maybe he's very hungry.*

A fun job

1 Grammar: Tina's Uncle Fred

Put in the adverbs.

1. He liked drawing *better* **(good)** than any other subject. He worked *hardest* **(hard)** at Art, harder than at all the other subjects together. He didn't do *well* **(good)** in some subjects, but in Maths he did *worse* **(bad)** than in the other subjects.
2. He draws important characters *more carefully* **(careful)** than less important ones and he works *most carefully* **(careful)** on the hero or heroine, of course! He draws less important characters *faster* **(fast)** than others.
3. Ideas for nasty characters come to him *more quickly* **(quick)** than for good ones.
4. He likes inventing new characters *best* **(good)** of all, because he can work *more freely* **(free)** and he can draw them as *imaginatively* **(imaginative)** as he likes.

2 Grammar: Comparisons

Make three different comparisons for each picture.

1 run • fast | 2 write • imaginative | 3 sing • bad

1. Donna runs fastest. She runs *faster than* Sally. Sarah doesn't run *as fast as* Sally and Donna.
2. Alan writes *most imaginatively*. He writes *more imaginatively than* José. Bruce doesn't write *as imaginatively as* José and Alan.
3. Peggy sings *worst*. She sings *worse than* Sue. Julie doesn't sing *as badly as* Sue and Peggy.

3 Grammar: Adjective or adverb?

Normally verbs are followed by adverbs, but some verbs are followed by adjectives. Complete the sentences with the correct form of the words on the right.

wonderful · fantastic · jealous · good · loud · nice · bad · angry

1. These flowers smell *wonderful/fantastic*.
2. Why do you laugh so *loudly*?
3. Your dress is beautiful. Everybody is looking at you *jealously*.
4. Are you ill? – Yes, I really feel *bad*.
5. Your pizza tastes absolutely *fantastic/wonderful*.
6. What's wrong? You look *angry*.
7. Tina's new boyfriend seems *nice*. I really like him.
8. Would you like to come to the cinema with me? – Yes. That sounds *good*.

4 Grammar: How are they doing it?

What are these people doing and how are they doing it? Use a different adverb in each sentence.

1. Tom and Huck are watching the gangsters nervously.
2. *Harry Potter is playing quidditch well/perfectly/brilliantly.*
3. *Lara Croft is training hard.*
4. *Mickey Mouse is jumping around crazily.*
5. *The Joker is running away from Batman quickly/fast.*
6. *Donald Duck is laughing loudly.*

The Native American Cinderella

1 Dictation: A costume for a party

13 Listen to track 13 and complete the text.

You can *easily make* a costume for a party, but *remember*: it must be *easy to wear*. If your costume is *too hot* or *not warm enough,* you *won't enjoy* the party. And think: *will you be able to sit down* in your costume? Can you *eat*, *drink and dance* in it? If you don't want people to *guess your identity*, then you will *have to wear* a mask. *However*, your friends will *recognize you* from the way you *walk and talk*. You can be *a character from a movie*, a book or a fairy story. Or you can be *really imaginative* and make a *version* of a *person from history*. The only thing *you can't be* is *invisible*.

2 Listening: A quiz about film characters

14 Listen to track 14. Then put the words in the right order and make sentences.

1. nasty • are • frogs • green • and
   Frogs *are green and nasty.*
2. time • the • all • and • broadly • smiles • is • he • black • white • and
   He *is black and white and smiles broadly all the time.*
3. man • world • character • is • this • the • in • strongest • the
   This *character is the strongest man in the world.*
4. magic • learns • he • school • he • student • is • where • a • at • a
   He *is a student at a school where he learns magic.*
5. nasty • about • green • angry • something • becomes • and • he • when • feels • he
   When *he feels angry about something he becomes green and nasty.*

Focus on traditions

1 Vocabulary: Definitions

Complete the definitions.

1. A ***mischievous*** person likes playing tricks on other people.
2. A ***Native American*** is another word for Indian.
3. A ***wizard*** uses ***magic*** to do fantastic things that other people can't do.
4. A ***fairy tale*** is a story which isn't true.
5. In a ***library*** you find many books.
6. ***Movie*** is another word for film.

2 Cloze test: Traditions

Fill in the gaps.

Four young people are talking about the ***cultural*** differences between their families' countries.

José: In our family ***traditions*** are very important. Mexican people don't only speak English, ***they*** speak Spanish, too. We also play traditional music ***on*** typical instruments in my dad's mariachi band. For the ***concerts***, my mum made me a real charro, our special ***costume***.

Tina: My family is Danish, but I don't know ***much*** about Denmark, the country of my great-great-grandparents. What I do ***know*** is that people there have big parties or ***celebrations*** for special events, e.g. the 50th wedding anniversary of ***my*** grandparents. We had so many wonderful cakes and ***I*** asked my grandma to give me some ***recipes*** because I wanted to try them at home and ***didn't*** know how to make them.

Donna: I'm from an Asian ***family*** and my parents have a restaurant because they ***love*** to cook the traditional food of their home ***country***. And their restaurant is always decorated with beautiful ***flowers***.

John: For a long time we weren't allowed to ***practice*** our traditions. But now one ***of*** the biggest Native American events is the Crow ***Fair*** in Montana, where you can see rodeos and ***parades*** with many people in colorful costumes, who move ***through*** the streets to celebrate.

GREEN LINE NEW

2

Bayern

2

Trainingsbuch Schulaufgaben

LEARNING ENGLISH GREEN LINE NEW

BAYERN

Das Lösungsheft ist
ein Bestandteil von
ISBN 978-3-12-**547271**-6

9 783125 472716